BODMIN
TEL. 2286

WADEBRIDGE
TEL. 2202

Padstow Library,
The Institute,
Padstow PL28 8AL
Tel. 532387

796.3340924

BODMIN M/L
Tel: 2286

18/11/7?

-9 FEB 1980

25 JUL 1981

17 AUG 1981

3 SEP 1981

30 SEP 1981

-9 FEB 1982

18 JUN 1982

27 AUG 1982

26 NOV 1982

8 FEB 1983

13 MAY 1983

-6. JAN. 84

1 JUN 1984

24 AUG 1984

-9. NOV. 1984

G000094917

it's all about a ball

it's all about a ball

an autobiography

Alan Ball

W.H.Allen · London
A Howard & Wyndham Company
1978

Copyright © Alan Ball, 1978

This book or parts thereof may not be
reproduced without permission in writing

Printed and bound in Great Britain by
Billing & Sons Limited
Guildford, London and Worcester
for the Publishers, W.H.Allen & Co. Ltd,
44 Hill Street, London, W1X 8LB

ISBN 0 491 02204 2

Dedication
To my family

Contents

PART I

From Farnworth to Wembley

Born to win

I was born on Victory Day – 12 May 1945 – which may have something to do with the fact that all my life I've wanted to be a winner.

Nothing else matters and everything I have ever done since has been geared to one objective. To be the best.

I'm not a bad sportsman, but I am a bad loser and I cannot understand the attitude of those who either don't want to win or think that coming second is acceptable as long as you've tried your best.

If your best isn't good enough to make you a winner get out of the game, that's my motto. I admit it's a motto that has landed me in more than my fair share of trouble, particularly with those in authority in English football.

Throughout my career I've been accused of opening my mouth too wide and too often. I've had verbal battles with managers, rows with the Football Association and League, arguments with referees and I've been a constant critic of the men in charge of English Soccer.

But I haven't done any of it for the sheer hell of it or because I like arguing. I'm not a little man who likes to attract attention by talking a lot. I reckon I have enough talent on the football field to attract all the attenion I need.

I talk a lot about the game because I feel so passionately about it. I criticise those in charge because, more than anything else, I want to see England on top.

I may still be a young man but, in football terms, I've

lived a lifetime. That is why I have written this book. I want to set the record right on many of the controversial issues in my career, to make it clear why I did what I did.

I have associated with most of the top personalities in football. Many of them I admire, some I hate. The same can be said about me – some love me, some despise me. But I don't think there are too many who can ignore me – you can't ignore winners.

I don't know what made me want to be a winner but I know those who helped me achieve that ambition, and those who tried to thwart me. During the course of this book I have tried to thank them or curse them as entertainingly and as accurately as possible.

A footballer's son

Southport has never been the greatest club in the Football League and is never likely to be. But it was on their ground, Haig Avenue, that my football ambitions began to take shape.

My father was playing for them just after the war and, as a lad of four, I used to sit in the dug-out and watch. He was only a part-timer. He did his job as a joiner during the week, trained in the evenings and played on Saturday.

But even at that age I knew he was different from the other kids' dads – and it was the football not the joinery that made him different. Before joining Southport he'd played for Birmingham and Oldham and, with all the confidence that four-year-olds possess, I knew I was going to be like him. I was going to play football for a living.

I was the smallest lad in the school at the village of Farnworth, just outside Bolton, where I was born and spent my early youth. But whenever it came to picking football teams during playtime I was always the first to be chosen.

We played with a tennis ball, like all other kids of that generation, but it didn't matter to me. Every game was vital, we had to win. It was my grandad Jimmy who gave me most encouragement during those early days.

He met me from school every day and he always had a ball with him. We'd swop passes all the way home and by the time I was six he was telling my father: 'Young Alan is going to be a better footballer than you are, mark my words.'

I think it was about then that my dad, realising that there were going to be two Alan Balls on the football scene, started calling himself 'Big Alan' and me 'Little Alan'.

I was a bright lad and had no trouble passing the 11-plus examination. But the only advantage of going to Grammar School as far as I was concerned was that they had better sporting facilities than the village school.

By this time my dad had moved into football management and was in charge of the non-League club Oswestry Town. That meant we moved with him and I went to Oswestry High School.

My academic record there might not stick in their memory but they'll probably remember the boy with red hair and little legs who used to win the cross-country every year. The longer the race the better I liked it. 'No-one is going to pass me,' I'd say to myself, and they seldom did. I also started amateur boxing and was a bit useful at that game.

My father's next managerial job was slightly different. He managed a pub, the Rose and Crown back at Farnworth. So off we went again and by now my mother and my younger sister Caroline had become used to these sudden upheavals.

All I can remember about life in a public house is that it

had a massive back-yard, ideal for football practice. And all I can remember about my new school, Farnworth Grammar, was that I won the cross-country there as well.

By now football was so much a part of my life that education was the last thing on my mind. The only homework I did was kicking a ball against the wall.

My grandfather had died when I was eleven and from then on my father took over my life completely.

My first real shirt

Now that I look back on it I don't think I made any decision of my own until I was eighteen or nineteen. I think my father wanted me to do well at school but, subconsciously, he was already planning my football career – and I was only too happy to follow.

Every Christmas and birthday the only presents I received were something to do with football. A football shirt, a pair of football boots or football stockings. Anything except the sort of presents the other kids were getting.

I was the proudest kid in the street when I received my first real football shirt. It was in black and white stripes, the colours of Newcastle United. They were the best team in England at the time – that's why my father chose it. Only the best for young Alan.

We didn't have a lot of money in those days but my mum also played her part in my football development by giving me the best food she could afford to build me up. At fourteen I was still only four foot tall and six stone wet through, but there wasn't a lad of my age who was tougher or fitter. My dad saw to that.

He always had only the white of the egg so that I could have an extra yolk. He ate the rind so I could have the bacon, I drank all the milk so he had black tea and I had enough cod-liver oil tablets shoved down me to make the whole village run.

But I had to repay his dedication by doing exactly as he told me and following his strict code of living.

I had a newspaper round and a bike was provided with the job. But my father wouldn't let me use the bike. I had to carry the heavy bags of paper and run from house to house delivering them. He used to time me and I was expected to go faster every week.

Because I never did any school homework I used to pay one of my friends' school bus fares so he would let me copy his homework. It meant I had no money to pay my own fare home so I had to run the five miles, but I figured it was good training and it never bothered me.

Just how far my father was prepared to go was illustrated by one incident I'll never forget. I had been bought a new pair of sandals and my mother had spent her last penny on them. The first day I wore them I kicked the crepe sole off playing football.

My mother was so upset that my dad gave me a belting and sent me to bed without any tea. As I lay in my room I heard him say to my mother: 'Valerie, give me that sandal. I'll try and mend it.'

Then suddenly I heard him yell out. 'Look, Valerie. It's his left shoe. He's kicking with his left foot, I've been trying to get him to do that for months.' I received an instant reprieve.

15

The trouble trail begins

I was still wearing short pants when I was sixteen, but in all other respects I was far more mature than the lads who used to take the mick out of me. I was playing senior football at the age of fifteen and had my first brush with authority – I was hauled before the Football Association.

By this time my dad had given up the pub and was now manager of another non-League club, Ashton United. The players were all semi-professionals, earning about £6 a week plus expenses, and my father had seen enough of my football to know that I was good enough to play in the team.

I more than held my own in that company and was really enjoying myself when someone studied the books at the end of the season and discovered that the players had been receiving more expenses than they should have been.

The club was reported to the FA and my dad and all the players were fined. It was the second time I had learnt that you couldn't do just what you liked in football.

When I was fourteen I had been playing for Wolverhampton Wanderers Junior side on Saturday mornings. It meant I had to make up all sorts of excuses to avoid playing for the school side. I think I went to sixteen weddings and eighteen funerals during six months.

But it was finally rumbled that I was not qualified to play for them and Wolves were reported to the FA. Their

16

manager, Stan Cullis, told me to come back when I was older.

But while my football education was moving ahead at a rapid pace my academic prowess was less impressive. In fact I was a dead loss. I took seven subjects in the GCE and failed the lot. But I didn't give a damn.

I had set my heart on being a footballer and as far as I was concerned anything else was a waste of time. It was then that I received a blow to my pride that left me completely shattered.

Remember, since the age of four I had put all my thought and effort into football. Now at the age of sixteen I was ready to fulfil those ambitions and everything that had happened so far led me to believe that it would be a mere formality.

I had signed for my local club, Bolton Wanderers, as an amateur and reckoned that all I had to do now was march into Burnden Park, tell them I'd left school and sign as a full-time professional.

I was ready to follow in the footsteps of those great Bolton stars, Nat Lofthouse and Bill Holden. But the Bolton manager Bill Ridding and his staff had other ideas. They started arguing about terms and finally one of them said: 'You're too small, son. You'd be better off trying to become a jockey.'

Someone else told my father: 'It would do your boy good to get his ankle broken. He holds the ball too much. He's too selfish.'

I couldn't believe my ears. I thought they were joking. I knew I was small, but that had never stopped me being the best player in any team I'd ever played with. I was better than all the other lads Bolton had given trials to and accepted and I knew it.

But Ridding remained unmoved. I was heartbroken when I got home but, as usual, expected my father to solve the problem. 'He'll find someone who will take me,' I thought. I was in for the second kick in the teeth in one day.

Instead of the sympathy and advice I expected, my father said: 'Well that's it, then. If Bolton don't want you

17

no-one will. You'd better get out and get yourself a job. And as you haven't got any qualifications from school it looks as if you're going to have to start as a labourer.'

It was like a nightmare. My dad, who had been behind me all the way, was now telling me to chuck the towel in. The tears were rolling down my face and for the first time in my life I had a go back at him.

'You're wrong, you're wrong. I'm going to be a foot-baller and I'm going to play for England before I'm twenty,' I screamed.

Then suddenly he leaned over, ruffled my hair and said: 'Alan, I've always known that. I just wanted to hear you say it and to know that you believe it. Don't worry, we'll find you a decent club to play for.' And he did.

A finger round fame

I've never been quite sure if my father did have any real plan in his mind when he made that promise or whether he was acting on sheer impulse, but soon after that Bolton setback we were on holiday in Blackpool when he said, 'Come on, we're going to see Ron Suart.'

He was the manager of Blackpool at the time and my dad had played with him in the past, so he walked in and asked him to give me a trial. What I didn't know at the time was that my father didn't want Suart to think that he had to do us a favour – so he told him that my name was Alan James.

He agreed to give me a trial and after watching me play

18

for only twenty minutes said, 'I've seen enough. You'll do for me.' I was ecstatic but there was still trouble ahead.

We went to Suart's office the following day to sign the forms and in walked Ray Parry, who had recently moved from Bolton to Blackpool for £25,000. He lived only two hundred yards from us and when he saw me he remarked, 'Hello, Alan, what are you doing here? Have you left Bolton?'

That did it. Ron Suart suddenly realised the lad he had given a trial to was not Alan James, but Alan 'James' Ball. And my dad had forgotten to explain that officially I was still an amateur at Bolton.

'Get out,' roared Suart. 'I can't have anything to do with you. We could be suspended by the FA for poaching.'

So back we went to Bolton to get my release and, luckily, when it was all legal Ron Suart eventually signed me. And I shall be eternally grateful to him. Even now, though I have played for four clubs, under many managers, I still call Ron Suart 'boss' whenever we meet.

He had given me my start and I knew that was all I needed. Once I'd got my little finger around fame I knew there was no way I was going to let go.

No-one worked harder than I did to learn everything there was to learn. I couldn't do enough training, I was always asking questions, eager to do anything asked of me.

Clean the boots, sweep out the dressing-rooms, collect the kit – if it was anything to do with football I was there beavering away.

But although I was subservient and respectful to all my elders off the field, my attitude changed completely once I stepped on to a football pitch. There, I reckoned, it was every man and boy for himself and I thought I was as good as any of them – or at least I was going to be.

And I wasn't ashamed to let people know what I thought, and that included everyone from the apprentices who worked alongside me to the biggest stars in the club, like the legendary Sir Stanley Matthews.

I was only eight when Matthews won his FA Cup medal in that famous Wembley match against Bolton in 1953 but here I was, at the age of sixteen, playing alongside him in practice matches. Most kids would have been so full of awe they'd have curled up and died rather than upset the great Matthews. But not me.

I was considered an orthodox right winger at that time and I knew that if I was going to get into the first team then it was Matthews I would have to replace. So I started saying to him, 'I'm going to take your place in this team soon.'

He looked at me in amazement. Until then I don't think he even knew I was there because he hadn't bothered to find out who I was.

I'd cleaned his boots and polished them so that you could see your face in them, but he never gave me a word of thanks or a shilling tip.

I made up my mind right then that when I did become a star, and I meant WHEN and not IF, I would look after the lads who were learning the game and I always have. And I also made up my mind that not even Sir Stanley was going to stand in my way.

He made it very clear that he was not pleased by this little red-haired upstart who kept chipping away at him every day. During one training session I played a great ball inside the full-back for him. He didn't even go for it but stopped and said to me: 'Son, in future you pass the ball to my feet. That's where I want it, AT MY FEET.'

That really got me going. 'Look,' I answered. 'When the ball is inside the full-back it's your job to bloody run and get it.'

Matthews went white with anger and shouted at Ron Suart, 'Take big-mouth off or I go off.' Suart took me off, but I think he admired me for the stand I'd made because it was not long afterwards that I was in that Blackpool first team.

The big break

I signed as a full-time professional with Blackpool on my seventeenth birthday and only three months later, in the first match of the 1962–63 season, I made my first team début – and what a début it was.

Matthews and Mandy Hill had both been injured in pre-season training and Suart decided that, despite my youth and inexperience, I was ready to be thrown in at the deep-end of professional football. And they don't come any deeper than Anfield, home of Liverpool who were then just starting their fantastic run of success.

They had been promoted to Division One the previous season and had gone right through that year without being beaten at home. When I knew I was actually going to be playing in front of 56,000 of the most fervent fans in football, I felt like Cinderella when she'd been told that she would go to the ball. It was a fairy tale right enough for me.

And, just like Cinderella, I got some smart new clothes for the occasion. My mother was worried that I wouldn't look right for the big day so she took me to Burton's on the morning of the match to buy me a new suit. I think my father was more nervous about my début than I was. He tried to be calm and professional about it by explaining that he couldn't come to see me play.

'Get out there and do your job. I've got mine to do' was

21

all he said, but I knew that deep down inside his stomach was doing cartwheels.

I couldn't have wished for a better start. We played brilliantly and won 2–1 and next morning I had all the headlines: 'Teenage Wonder' and all that bit. I loved every minute of the match and every word of the publicity.

'This is for me,' I thought. 'This is what I have always dreamed of.' And I knew at that moment that nothing was going to stop me now. I knew that I was going to the very top. It was all there in front of me, I only had to put out my hand and grasp it.

I also knew I still had things to learn, but I had people around to help. Apart from my father, there were people at Blackpool who, luckily, did not think the way Matthews did. Men like Ray Parry, Bruce Crawford, Pat Quinn, Eric Haywood, Bobby Finen, Harry Cummins and Jack Duckworth.

I still remember making a car journey with Ray Parry and Bruce Crawford, during which they gave me a few home truths about 'selfish' footballers.

As you can gather I was a cocky kid with plenty to say for myself. It didn't do me any harm and I still admire youngsters like it today if they have the ability and the ambition. But there are also times when the young and the brash can get carried away and need a sharp reminder. Parry and Crawford gave me that all right.

'The next time I work my guts out to get into space when you've got the ball I expect to bloody well get the ball, not to see you try and beat every other player in the team,' said Parry.

Then Crawford piled in, 'You have got a lot of talent lad and you'll go a long way. But remember, you can't win a football match on your own, no matter how good you are. You are going to need the rest of the team and if you don't give the ball to them, they're not going to give it to you.'

It was one of the biggest roastings I'd had in my life until then, and it's a lesson I've never forgotten.

And just to underline the fact that I was still only on the threshold of the big-time Ron Suart dropped me after a run of five first-team matches.

We were beaten 5–0 at Ipswich and although I knew that the defeat was certainly not my fault I was the one who got the chop.

'You've got a great future but we don't want to rush you. ...' 'Too many games now will be bad for your development, you're still growing. ...' 'I think you're good enough to play but with a bit more experience behind you you'll be even better. ...'

I must have heard all those excuses trotted out at least a hundred times during the rest of that season, but I never did get another first-team game during it. It was frustrating but now that I look back I know they were right to hold me back. I still had a lot of the basics to learn and with Bobby Finen in charge of the reserve team I had a great tutor.

The message

There is something in my character that makes me react to someone who I feel is willing me to do well. I want to be loved in the sense that I need to know all the time that someone cares what I am doing, is happy that I am succeeding, is glad to have me on their side.

I have played for many managers who gave me that feeling, and a few who were the exact opposite. I shall be writing about them later, but the first man, apart from my father, who made me want to play for him was Bobby Finen.

We were only playing reserve football in the Central

League but he made them all vital and his enthusiasm carried over to me. It was during that spell under Bobby that I think I grew up as a footballer and by the time the following season started I was ready to fulfil my role in life.

In fact, the first game of that 1963–64 season was one I will always remember, although it was only an unimportant friendly against Preston.

My father was watching and so was my Uncle Trevor, who is one of my biggest fans and has travelled all over the world to see me play.

I can't even remember what the result was, but I suddenly felt everything click into place. As I left the field I knew I was ready, my apprenticeship was over and I wasn't the only one who knew it.

Dad never said anything, but as I came off he gave me that half-smile which meant everything. 'You'll do, son,' was the message that came over loud and clear.

I didn't get into the first team for the opening three matches but then they lost 6–1 at Old Trafford. I was immediately brought into the side and the following week we beat Manchester United at home. I had finally arrived and I was never dropped again.

But although I was now a regular member of a top First Division side, the glamour that most people associate with the life of a football star who is unattached and living in a lively place like Blackpool was still not for me. My dad saw to that.

I was living in digs during my time at Blackpool with a lovely old lady called Mrs Mawson. Sharing them with me were Emlyn Hughes and Hugh Fisher – two future England captains in the same boarding house can't be a bad record.

But, although I was away from home for the first time, my father's influence was always there – sitting on my shoulder, making sure I never made a move that might in any way affect my one aim in life. To be a star.

It would have been very easy to have lived the sort of life most lads of seventeen or eighteen can only dream about.

24

There I was, a celebrity in a town where there are more girls to the square mile than almost any other in England.

But the only Blackpool lights I saw were the floodlights at the ground. When the girls came chasing I started running. My dad had laid down the rules before I left home and I stuck to them as rigidly as Moses did to the Ten Commandments.

No girls – except Lesley

I was in bed by nine-thirty every night. I drank nothing that even looked liked alcohol. I wouldn't even talk to anyone who was smoking a cigarette and, the biggest rule of all was – NO GIRLS.

That last rule was easy to obey because back home when I was fifteen I had met a girl named Lesley Newton. She was a friend of my sister Caroline, who is two years younger than me.

Lesley used to come around to our house to see Caroline, but after a time she saw more of me than my sister. She was the only girlfriend I ever had, because I never went anywhere else to meet other girls.

And, because my dad never suspected that romance would blossom right under his own nose, he never realised what was happening.

After I had left home and moved to Blackpool I continued to see Lesley, but I would never allow her to meet my father now that she had become my girlfriend. We were courting for two years while I was a Blackpool player

– but it was probably one of the strangest courtships of all time.

We saw each other twice a week during those two years but always at my digs where we played records most nights. We never went out because I was afraid we would be seen and the word would get back to dad. She never came to see me play, and we used to say goodnight at nine so that I could get to bed by nine-thirty.

The rest of the team thought that being young and single I was out on the town every night and couldn't understand why I was always raring to go in training every morning.

The first time my father suspected what was going on was when Ron Suart invited my parents to see one of our matches and put them up at the biggest hotel in Blackpool.

But instead of going to the hotel to see them after the game I slipped off to meet Lesley. My father couldn't understand where I was and when someone finally told him I had gone to the cinema with a girlfriend he refused to believe it.

'Alan wouldn't go out with a girl. There must be something wrong with him,' he said, and proceeded to spend the rest of the night ringing every hospital in the area.

Finally I admitted to him that I was very serious about Lesley but, even though I was now eighteen, he didn't like it. When I took her home he refused to talk to her and acted as if she wasn't there.

When I was nineteen we got engaged. I was too scared to tell my father but the rest of the family knew and it was my grandmother who finally let it slip. She got so excited she put a message of congratulation in the local paper. My dad saw it and went crazy.

But that was nothing to his reaction when I decided to get married a year later. 'You must be bloody mad. What do you want to get tied down with a wife and kids for? You can have the world,' he shouted.

Then, just before the wedding, he invited me out for a drink. I thought that at last he had accepted what I was doing, but dad doesn't give in that easily.

26

He had spent weeks building up a dossier on Lesley and he now presented it to me. He'd managed to get all sorts of people to say she was no good for me, even friends of ours.

He had dug really deep and listed hundreds of reasons why I shouldn't marry her. But I knew it was a load of nonsense and there was nothing he could find against Lesley. So we had another row.

I think what really upset him was the fact that, for the first time in my life, I was making a major decision without his advice or consent. He knew that from now on I was going to be my own man.

He came to the wedding and, for the first time, was sociable to Lesley.

'A bloody prima donna'

Even then dad had the last laugh. We were married on 21 May 1967, nine days after my twenty-second birthday. And our honeymoon lasted exactly one day.

Because the next day I had to report to Sir Alf Ramsey and his squad for an international against Spain at Wembley followed by a three-week international tour.

And even when I was well and truly wed my father made it clear that, when it came to football, he was still the guiding influence in my career. He had seen me become one of the best players in Britain and he was not about to let me throw it all away. If ever I showed any sign of breaking the rigid code of conduct on or off the field that he had set me, he would suddenly arrive from nowhere to let me know he was still watching. I'll never forget one of those encounters.

I was an England player, the star of Everton and very much a married man when my father pulled his next extraordinary trick.

Lesley and I arrived home late one Saturday night. I had played that day but I was going through a bad patch and the crowd had given me some stick. When we arrived in the house I was staggered to see my father waiting for me.

I said: 'Hello dad, it's great to see you ...' but he cut me short.

'Don't give me all that good-to-see-you stuff,' he said. 'Look at the bloody time. It's two-thirty in the morning and here's you, playing like a mug but still going out and enjoying yourself.

'I saw you laughing and joking like a couple of kids. You're living in bloody fairyland, son. You know what you've become don't you. A bloody prima donna.'

I was staggered and confused. I didn't even know he'd been at the match. He was manager of Preston at the time but he had forsaken his own team to come and watch me, paying at the turnstiles and standing with the fans on the terraces – the same fans who had been giving me the bird. No wonder he was angry.

I wanted to throw my arms around him and tell him how sorry I was for letting him down.

I knew how hard it had been for him to come and act the way he had. But I also knew why he had to do it. He had taught me all my life to fight for my football future and he was teaching me now that I still had to fight if I wanted to remain at the top.

I had plenty to think about after he left that night. The following home match at Goodison Park I was still struggling to find my form, but no-one could have tried harder. I chased everything, fought for every ball and even got booked for arguing.

That night, when Lesley and I got home, my father was waiting again. He came towards me and I instinctively ducked, expecting another right-hander. Instead he put his

28

arms around me, hugged me and said: 'You were still rubbish out there today but at least you were fighting again. Keep that up and in three weeks you'll be playing as well as ever again.'

As usual he was right and, luckily, I've never had another spell in my career like that. If I had I'm sure my old man would have been back swinging punches.

Record fee

It must be fairly evident by now who has had the most effect on my life and career. My father is the king, without him I'd have been nothing. But other men have played their part in shaping my Soccer outlook and one of them was the man I played under after leaving Blackpool. It was Harry Catterick, manager of Everton.

Blackpool had been a great club for me and I never had any quarrel with Ron Suart who had given me my start. But although I was happy there, the world was beginning to look bigger to me.

At that time I was an England star with a World Cup winner's medal and I knew a lot of top clubs were watching me. I had asked for a transfer in July 1965 and again a year later, when I refused to re-sign the new contract Blackpool had offered me.

There had been a great deal of speculation in the newspapers. Every day there were stories saying I was going to Leeds or Manchester United or Everton.

I didn't pay too much attention to any of them. I was content to sit back and let my future run its course, wherever it happened to lead me. I think that with a better contract I'd have been quite happy to stay with Blackpool.

But when the break did come it was with a startling suddenness. One day I was sitting in a Blackpool coffee bar with Hughie Fisher our wing-half and the next I was the costliest player in British football, valued at £110,000.

I'd gone to the coffee bar after a training session when a message came saying Ron Suart wanted to see me in his office immediately.

When I arrived he simply said: 'Harry Catterick is outside. He wants to sign you.'

'What do you think about it?' I asked him.

'I would prefer it if you signed for him,' he replied.

The way he put the accent on the word *him* left me in no doubt that other clubs had made offers but that Suart, for some reason, was not happy with them.

I went out to meet Catterick and felt immediately comfortable with the man. He didn't have to sell Everton to me. I knew it was one of the best clubs in England. I knew they had a good side that was getting better and I knew the atmosphere at Goodison Park would suit me down to the ground. They had big gates every week and I have always responded to large crowds – and the more fanatical they are, the better. I knew there were not many more fanatical fans than those on Merseyside.

I phoned my father to ask his advice but there was never any real doubt in my mind that I would sign – and I never had any regrets about that move.

Everton lived up to all my expectations. I scored in my first match for them at Fulham, and I loved every minute of my five seasons with them. I won a League championship medal, reached the FA Cup final only to be beaten by West Bromwich Albion, got to two other FA semi-finals and also to the quarter-final of the European Cup.

That's not a bad record and, most important to Everton fans, it was a better record than Liverpool's during those five years. The rivalry between the Anfield and Goodison fans is fantastic. I couldn't go anywhere in Liverpool without being cheered by our lot or jeered by the other lot. But I never experienced any malice.

Neither side will ever admit it, but their rivalry is based on respect. I'd have been far more worried if the Liverpool fans didn't have a go at me. If you're ignored it means they do not consider you a threat.

And, of course, there was always Bill Shankly around to liven the relationships between the two clubs. There have been hundreds of stories told about Shankly, but I think it relevant at this point to tell my favourite story about him.

During the season we won the championship – 1969–70 – we had lost 3–0 at Goodison Park but played Liverpool at home in a match that was vital to us in our title chase. We won at Anfield 2–0, and while we were overjoyed it was obvious Shanks was upset that his greatest rivals should have taken a step nearer the crown.

Normally, Shankly was always waiting at the tunnel as the teams came off and he usually had a word for players of both teams. But this time there was no sign of him. We found it strange, because Shanks is not the sort to hide, whatever has happened to his team.

But about fifteen minutes later there was a knock on our dressing-room door and, sure enough, there was Shankly. In that thick Scots accent of his he said: 'Congratulations, boys, but I just want to point out one thing. We beat you 3–0 at Goodison Park and you won 2–0 tonight. You might take the title, but on aggregate it's 3–2 to us this season and that makes us winners in any competition you care to mention in the world.'

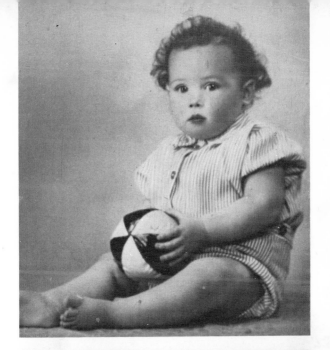

SYNDICATION INTERNATIONAL LIMITED

top: Baby Alan with a firm grip on the ball. *bottom:* Alan Ball Senior as manager of Preston.

SYNDICATION INTERNATIONAL LIMITED

Homecoming – after being sent off against Poland. But wife, Lesley and daughter Keely are a great consolation.

SYNDICATION INTERNATIONAL LIMITED

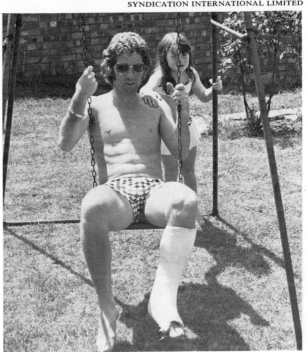

top: Daughter Keely toasts new brother Jimmy. *bottom:* Swinging a broken leg with eldest daughter, Mandy.

DAILY MIRROR. KENT GAVIN

Two England Captains relax – the tall one is cricketer Tony Greig.

THE PRESS ASSOCIATION

Another Ball winner, Gargon Prince canters home.

BLACKPOOL FOOTBALL CLUB

v.

WOLVERHAMPTON W.

FOOTBALL LEAGUE

SATURDAY, 25th AUGUST, 1962

Kick-off 3.0 p.m.

OFFICIAL PROGRAMME

PRICE - THREEPENCE

BLACKPOOL—Tangerine and White   **FOOTBALL LEAGUE**

1—WAITERS

RIGHT   2—ARMFIELD   3—MARTIN   LEFT

4—CRAWFORD   5—GRATRIX   6—DURIE

7—BALL   8—GREEN   9—CHARNLEY   10—PARRY   11—HORNE

Referee:
    Mr. A. ATHERTON (Runcorn)

Linesmen:
    Mr. A. ENTWISTLE (Red Flag)
    Mr. J. D. JONES (Yellow Flag)

NEXT HOME MATCH:

MONDAY NEXT, 27th AUGUST

Central League

BURY RESERVE

Kick-off 7.30 p.m.

11—HINTON   10—MURRAY   9—FARMER   8—CROWE   7—WHARTON

6—FLOWERS   5—WOODFIELD   4—GOODWIN

LEFT   3—THOMSON   2—SHOWELL   RIGHT

1—DAVIES

WOLVERHAMPTON W.   Kick-off 3.0 p.m.

Breaking into the big time – Alan's name appears in the Blackpool's First team programme for the first time, 25 August, 1962.

POST OFFICE

TELEGRAM

Prefix. Time handed in. Office of Origin and Service Instructions. Words.

OFFICE STAMP

No._____

arges to pay
___s.____d.
RECEIVED

_____m   At _____m
N

30 2.0 NANTWICH ST RETRANS LHX 12 =

BALL BLACKPOOL FC C/O LIVERPOOL FC ANFIELD LIVERPOOL

= PROUD OF YOU = DAD + +

For free repetition of doubtful words telephone "TELEGRAMS ENQUIRY" or call, with this form
at office of delivery. Other enquiries should be accompanied by this form, and, if possible, the envelope.   B or C.

PROUDER +   MRO 11 + =

pay
___s.____d.
RECEIVED

No._____
OFFICE ST.

TELEGRAM

Prefix. Time handed in. Office of Origin and Service Instructions. Words.

_____m   74   At _____
M27 12.50 WILMSLOW 11 =   To _____
                                           By _____

ALAN BALL ENGLAND DRESSING ROOM WREXHAM F/C

WREXHAM =

PROUDER STILL = DAD +

For free repetition of doubtful words telephone "TELEGRAMS ENQUIRY" or call, with this form
at office of delivery. Other enquiries should be accompanied by this form, and, if possible, the envelope.   B or C

The telegrams that meant so much, *top:* August 1962, *bottom:* November 1964.

PRESTON ENTERPRISES

LONDON & ESSEX GUARDIAN NEWSPAPERS

top: Alan poses with the beauty queens during his Everton Days. *bottom:* The lads he coached at Harlow.

The hard man who cared

Good old Shanks! It had taken him fifteen minutes to think that one up but he left our dressing-room well-pleased with himself. And why not?

Shankly is my sort of man. He has a passion for the game, the sort of passion my father has, the sort of passion I inherited. And Shanks always does what he believes to be right. That's the most important thing.

And it's one of the qualities I also admired in Harry Catterick. He did not have the same bubbling personality as Shankly but he cared just as much about his club and his team.

And he was one of the hardest men I've ever played under. He ruled by fear in many ways. There were times when I was really scared of that man. He'd do anything to get results.

He's the only manager I've ever known who made his players sign a book when they arrived at the ground in the morning, and you had to write down what time you arrived. It was just like clocking in at a factory – and you were fined for every minute you were late.

He also got more agitated than any other manager I've known. If we'd had a bad match the next practice session was murder. He'd lock the doors at the training ground and no-one got out until he was satisfied that we'd worked well enough and hard enough. It was like a prison camp at times.

But if you gave Catterick the results he expected he could also be the most generous man in the business.

I remember when we reached the FA Cup final against West Bromwich in 1968. There had been some trouble over tickets issued to players getting into the hands of spivs when Everton met Sheffield Wednesday in the 1966 final.

Now the Everton board decided to clamp down on us. We were told that we would be getting only twelve tickets each.

You can imagine the uproar that caused – it wouldn't even be enough to get our close relatives into Wembley, never mind the million friends you suddenly find at Cup Final time.

As captain it was my responsibility to go and see Catterick and tell him the players were not too happy about the situation. I wasn't looking forward to it – as I said, Catterick could be a hard man to argue with. But he listened to what I had to say and answered: 'You're quite right. It isn't enough. Leave it to me.' We all got as many tickets as we wanted.

If I saw the generous side of his nature that day I saw the cold, clinical side of his character when he called me into his office in December, 1971, and said, without any trace of emotion: 'You're up for sale. You can go.'

I told him I didn't want to leave, that I still loved Everton. He just said: 'There's a man in the next room from a top London club. It will be a good move for you and you'll make some money out of the transfer fee. I want you to sign for him.'

It was then that I realised what sort of game football really is. It's a business in which players are moved around like slaves. I must admit I became very cynical about life that day, but in my heart I had to admire Catterick and I certainly had no animosity towards him.

The Arsenal style

Catterick had bought me for £110,000 and now he was selling me five years later at the age of twenty-six for £220,000. That's got to be good business and he was quite right to do the deal. It was a professional move and I always admire good professionals.

And so I went into the next room to meet the man from London who was paying another British record fee for me – Bertie Mee of Arsenal.

You couldn't find two men more different in outlook than Catterick and Mee. The Arsenal manager was a real gentleman. He was not a soccer tactician by any stretch of the imagination, but he was always willing to listen to his players and he surrounded himself with good coaches. He let them sort out the tactics – he got on with running the club.

And he did it brilliantly. I had heard so much about the great Arsenal when I was a lad. The greatest club in the world, the marble halls, a tradition second to none.

I certainly wasn't disappointed, it lived up to all those descriptions. When Arsenal travel to away matches, either at home or abroad, they do it in style. It's the best of everything and they really make their players feel important.

Most clubs rush back from away games as quickly and as cheaply as possible. Not Arsenal.

The coach they travelled in had just about everything.

There was waiter service and three-course meals. Anything you wanted was available, smoked salmon, beef salads, every drink you could think of and cigars – even After-Eight mints. It was luxury all the way down the line and that applied to foreign trips where it was Champagne service on the flight and only the best hotels.

When I told the England players the sort of service we used to get at Arsenal they wouldn't believe me.

It was December, 1971, when I moved to Arsenal, the season after they had achieved the Championship and FA Cup double. It was, perhaps, a bad time to join them. They were looking for a new team and a new style and they also had to try and live up to that double success – an almost impossible task.

I was desperate to help them win something, not just for my sake but for Bertie Mee who had gambled on me. I think he was criticised at the time for spending so much on me and I wanted to help him justify it.

But after some near misses it became increasingly obvious that we were getting worse instead of better. By the end of the 1974–75 season I was becoming more restless and disillusioned.

I could see things that needed to be done to improve the team but nothing was happening. I didn't want to take over but I thought that my ideas were worth listening to.

In the end I decided that the only way to make my point was to ask for a transfer. I didn't really want to leave and I still had great respect for Bertie Mee and his coach Bobby Campbell. I thought that my request would shake Mee into action, that the board would want to know my reasons for leaving and we could get something going again.

It was about this time that Don Revie had recalled me to the England team and made me captain, and there were many who said I was just trying to cash in on this by getting a move while I was England skipper.

That was nonsense. Bobby Campbell was perhaps the only one at that time who knew how I felt and it was he who finally persuaded me to stay at Highbury. I knew I could work well with Bobby. He is probably one of the best coaches in England, always aware of what players are

36

trying to do and always ready to listen and discuss tactical problems with them, unlike so many of our coaches who are stubborn and very narrow in their outlook.

Once Campbell had convinced me that my future was still with Arsenal I wrote to the chairman asking to come off the transfer list and telling him that it was all my fault and that it had nothing to do with Bertie Mee. I've never been too proud to admit a mistake and I also knew Bertie was under some pressure from the board. I didn't want him to carry the can for me.

Neill's cowboys

When Mee finally resigned as Arsenal manager it was a sad day for me, but there was an even sadder one to come. I, and many other players at the club, were convinced that Bobby Campbell would get Mee's job – we even had a meeting at which we voted unanimously to let the board know the way we felt about him.

Instead, they opted for Terry Neill, the former Arsenal centre-half who was then managing Tottenham. In my opinion it was a bad move. The players, particularly the young ones, all had great respect for Campbell, but it soon became obvious that Neill had none of his qualities, he quickly fell out with many of the playing staff.

In our first training session under Neill I recall he stood behind the goal and threw the ball over the bar towards us.

We had to run and side-foot it into the net from about eight yards with no goalkeeper there. When he was sure we

37

could all do that he changed tactics – we then had to head the ball into the net.

I felt a complete fool. Any six-year-old could have done that. 'If my dad could see me now he'd think I'd gone mad,' I remember thinking to myself.

He brought with him his assistant, Wilf Dixon, who is a very nice man. But, tactically, neither of them could compare with Campbell or any of the coaches at Arsenal in recent years. In fact, they don't compare favourably with any of the coaches I've ever played under.

We had an early view of Neill's approach when he took us on a pre-season tour soon after joining us in the summer of 1976. We were in Zurich and before the match Neill called for a team talk.

He carried a bag into the meeting and from it he took a handful of toy cowboys, all in various shooting poses with their pistols and rifles. 'This is us,' he said, laying them out on the table. Then he took out another handful of toys. These were all Red Indians. He threw them in a pile on the table surrounded by the cowboys. 'And that's the opposition,' he said. 'We'll destroy them just like that.'

I don't know how I stopped laughing out loud and when I looked around the rest of the team were also trying to keep their sniggers to themselves. 'What a disaster this is going to be,' I thought.

It didn't take me long to get into Neill's black book either. On that same tour he ordered us to train on Sunday morning after a match on the Saturday.

'There's no way I'm going training on a Sunday,' I said to Peter Storey. 'Me neither,' he said, and off we went to a local café for our Sunday lunch and a few glasses of wine. Neill was very upset about it, but he never said a word to us himself. Instead he sent the club secretary, Ken Friar, to find us and tell us of his displeasure.

He didn't even fine us. Instead he stored the memory away for further use, like the time when he was ready to sell us. Peter Storey went to Fulham and I moved to Southampton and that was before Neill's first season was half over.

The final crunch between Neill and myself came in the

quarter-final of the League Cup against Queen's Park Rangers. It was an important match for the players and also for Neill – he saw chances of winning a major trophy in his first season with the club and we needed to win something to boost our morale.

But during the team talk Neill insisted that he wanted Trevor Ross to mark their schemer, Don Masson, and he wanted me to run free. I disagreed violently.

I argued that I should mark Masson. I have great respect for young Ross but felt that I had more experience and could do a better job. And I knew if we put Masson out of the game we could win it.

Neill wouldn't listen and insisted that we use his plan. But as we ran on to the field I said: 'Take no notice Trevor. I'm marking Masson, you go free.'

And that's what we did and it worked like a dream. Pat Rice scored an early goal, Masson never got a kick and just before half-time we were awarded a penalty that would have wrapped it up for us. I missed it.

I obviously wasn't happy with myself, no-one likes missing penalties, but I was still pleased with the way the game was going and thought we had a great chance of winning.

But at half-time Neill went mad. Not because of the penalty but because I had disobeyed his order about Masson. 'But it's working,' I said.

'I don't care. You do what I tell you,' he answered. So we played it his way and in the second half Rangers took over and beat us 2–1. That was the last straw for me. I knew I could never play for this man.

He didn't help matters with his outbursts to the Press about the team. After we had won at Coventry he stormed into the dressing-room, told us we had played rubbish football, should never have won and generally gave us a real roasting.

He then went and told the Press the same thing. We were staggered. We knew we hadn't played all that well, but what the hell, we had won. We'd played brilliantly at times and been beaten, it was swings and roundabouts to us and we expected Neill to take the same attitude.

He followed this up soon after by saying on television that we were all morons. I couldn't let that one go by unchallenged. At Monday's team meeting I told him exactly what I thought about him. I said he had no right to say that about any player, that he could never expect their respect if he didn't respect them.

Turks or Saints

I told him what I thought of his tactics — or his lack of them — and that as far as I was concerned he knew what he could do with his football team.

He just looked at me and said, 'I'm not here for you to love me.'

I'll say this for Neill. He'd make a good Public Relations man and I reckon before he's finished he will have charmed football directors all over the world. In the end the parting of the ways came quickly.

He called me in and said, 'You've got your way. You're up for sale.'

I asked which clubs were interested and he said: 'One in America and one in Turkey. I'm checking on the flight times now to get you on a plane to Istanbul.'

I thought he was joking but he was dead serious. I asked him what the fee was but he wouldn't tell me. I later discovered that he wanted £100,000 if I went abroad and £60,000 from an English club, but I can't believe that was ever authorised by the Arsenal board.

In the end I had a choice of five clubs – the Americans, the Turks, Blackpool, Leeds and Southampton.

I wasn't really interested in going abroad, although they were both good offers – particularly from Istanbul. But I had my children's future to think of.

Jimmy Armfield at Leeds was very persuasive but all he could offer me was medals. I'm not a greedy man but you have to get what you can while you can in this game and Armfield made it clear there would be no increase in my pay packet if I moved to Leeds.

Blackpool made me a good offer which I might have accepted if I had not met Lawrie McMenemy of Southampton. When I arrived he took me into his office, locked the door and said: 'You're signing for Southampton and you're not getting out of here until you do.'

I liked his style, I liked his terms and I have had no regrets about joining him. He has ambition and he is not afraid to go out and buy the players he thinks will achieve those ambitions.

And, having bought them, he is not afraid to listen to what they have to say and to make use of their experience.

We had some great training sessions and team talks at Southampton. Peter Osgood and Ted MacDougall have, like myself, both been about in this game. We've all picked up a lot of useful information on our travels.

McMenemy never reached the heights as a player but, unlike some managers I know, he doesn't resent that fact. He is always prepared to listen and learn. You get some men who, because they never made it big as a player, try their hardest to belittle the guys who have.

They're for ever telling you that they were unlucky. They'd have been great but for this injury or that unlucky break. McMenemy knows his limitations but makes up for it with his attitude to management.

After only a few weeks at Southampton I noticed what I thought was a weakness in the team. I mentioned it to Lawrie and the next day he had us working on it in training, asking other players for their opinions on my theory. Once we'd worked on it he decided to give it a go in our next League match. It was a disaster and we were hammered 3–0 at Blackburn. Many managers would have dropped the plan immediately. But McMenemy decided to give it another try.

In the following game against Oldham at home we won 4–0 and everyone agreed that the new system worked. As far as I'm concerned that makes everything worthwhile. That's what football is all about.

The last fence

I've won a World Cup winner's medal and a Football League championship medal, but I reckon that I am jinxed when it comes to the FA Cup.

It is one of the greatest competitions in Soccer, nothing makes players try harder or gives supporters a bigger thrill than the thought to getting to Wembley at the end of the season for that great day – Cup Final day.

I have been fortunate to be there twice as a player on that day – and I have two loser's medals to show for those visits. But I am very proud of them, because I was glad just to be at Wembley on those two occasions.

There are thousands of players right now who would be happy just to be guaranteed a place in the sixth round and even more who would give anything for a place in the semi-final.

Of course, it hurts to get so far and to lose out at the last fence. But the experience of being there just outweighs the winning. It is one of the few occasions in my sporting life when I've had to admit that it's better to have played in it and lost than never to have played in it at all.

Perhaps I should have realised early on that the FA Cup was going to be my unlucky competition. In the three years I was with Blackpool we never got past the third round.

And, judging by my experiences since, Southampton should have been a good bet to get to the final in 1978 – and LOSE.

Because Everton won the Cup by beating Sheffield Wednesday in 1966. I joined them the following season and in 1968 they reached the final again – but were beaten by West Bromwich Albion.

Arsenal won the Cup with a win over Liverpool in 1971. Then I joined them and they reached the final again, only to be beaten by Leeds.

And Southampton won the Cup in 1976 with their win over Manchester United. The following year I joined them so, as you can see, they are due for a return visit but with my jinx they won't win it.

Although I've said I was not ashamed of those loser's medals, at the time I collected the first of them I admit I didn't care if they gave it to me or not, in fact I threw it on the floor in disgust. Luckily, it was retrieved for me because I quickly regretted that impulsive action. But it had been a frustrating experience losing that game to West Bromwich by the only goal of the match which was scored by Jeff Astle.

We were considered certainties to win the game and not without good cause. In two League fixtures that season we had beaten Albion 5–3, a match in which I scored two goals, and 6–2, and in that one I scored four times.

So you can imagine how I felt losing to them in the one that mattered. But that's the beauty of the FA Cup. Should Sunderland have beaten Leeds? Should Southampton have triumphed over Manchester United? It's full of surprises and upsets and I was just unlucky enough to be on the wrong end of one of them that day.

The losers' dressing-room at Wembley is always a sad place, but perhaps ours was not as bad as most after that defeat. Five of the team had a winner's medal from two

43

years earlier and as Harry Catterick told the rest of us, 'You're all young enough and good enough to be back next year.'

But it was four years before I was to get my second chance, and that was with Arsenal. The previous season they had won the double and had beaten Liverpool at Wembley. Everyone was confident that, although the powerful Leeds side was the opposition this time, another double was on the way – two successive Final triumphs.

There were only two changes in the Arsenal side from that Liverpool victory. Geoff Barnett was in goal instead of the injured Bob Wilson, and I replaced Ray Kennedy who was on the subs bench.

But again I was on the losing side, and once more beaten by the only goal of the match. The lone consolation I have is that it was a particularly fine goal from Allan Clarke.

There was nothing between the two sides on the day and those of us out in the middle thought it was a good match for the spectators, but it seems that on that score we were wrong, few of them enjoyed the match as a spectacle.

So once more I climbed the steps to the Royal Box to collect my loser's medal and once more I was one of the few men in the dressing-room to feel let down. The others had a winner's medal at home to absorb the blow.

But I would not have missed those experiences for the world. I've also suffered the fate of being beaten in the semi-final, and that's the worst fate of all because the best part of reaching the final is the build-up to it.

It still haven't given up hope of finally ending my hoodoo and getting a winner's medal at Wembley to give me a personal treble, World Cup, Championship and FA Cup medal.

That's the greatest thing of all about the FA Cup. Every year it gives every player, from the lowest to the highest, something to dream about, and I'm still in there dreaming with the rest of them.

Forgotten heroes

There is another award open to players that has not come my way – the Footballer of the Year award. But ten years ago I was quoted as saying: 'If I was voted the Footballer of the Year I would not accept it.' I still feel the same way.

It is not that I do not respect the people who make the award, the Football Writers' Association, it's just that I think the whole thing is based on the wrong values. The winner is invariably a player who comes from the team that has won the championship or has reached the FA Cup final.

I have no intention of taking anything away from those who have received the award and have proudly accepted it. That is their prerogative. But a player can have a fantastic season with great impact on the game yet because his team finishes second in the League and is beaten in the Cup semi-final the chances are he will not win the award. I think that's crazy.

And I do not confine my criticism to the football writers only. I think the footballers themselves fall into the same trap. They now have the PFA award for the 'Players' Player of the Year.' There is no way that should be equated to success in a competition during the season.

The players should be more aware than anyone that the best men in their profession, by that I mean hard-working, fair, honest and dedicated players, don't always win the medals. Respect for a player's character as well as his ability should be the test when voting time comes around.

Another pet hate I had as a younger player was that I refused to talk about football with anyone who was not connected with the game.

I think this came about after a series of encounters with the more ignorant section of the football-watching public. You know the type, he always asks you a question and gives you the answer at the same time.

'So-and-so is the best player in England, isn't he, Alan?' or 'This is the best team in the League, wouldn't you say, Alan?'

Then, if you don't happen to agree with them, they start hurling abuse at you. There was a time when I tried to argue with them, but quickly learned it got me nowhere. They just were not prepared to be convinced. I don't know why they asked for my opinion in the first place if they didn't respect it.

That's when I went through the period of just ignoring these characters. But I discovered that by making that a blanket rule I was often offending people who were genuine, loved their football and were willing to listen and learn.

I try to be more tolerant now, but if possible I would still prefer to confine my soccer chats to the men in the game and talk about other aspects of life with the rest.

PART II
Ramsey, Revie and England

Alf Ramsey

On the last day of the 1973–74 season I broke my leg playing for Arsenal against Queen's Park Rangers. In the same week Alf Ramsey got the sack as England team manager.

It was obviously a sad, emotional time for him but what did the man do? He sat down and wrote me a letter. He told me not to worry about my leg because he knew I had all the qualities to overcome such a setback. He said that he was sure it would not affect my international career and wished me the best possible luck and success in the future.

I almost cried when I read it. It was so typical of the man to think about his players while he was in trouble himself. It was typical, also, of his dealings with me from the first moment we met.

That was when he chose me for an England Under-23 match against Wales at Wrexham in November, 1964. I was only too delighted to get recognition at the age of nineteen.

But when I turned up to report he met me and thanked me for coming. As if I needed any thanks. I'd have paid to play.

I don't think there was ever a sour moment in our relationship from that day onwards. And I think almost all the great things that have happened to me during my career revolve around Alf.

Like my first senior international. I had lived with that

dream and the promise given to my father when I left school that I would play for England before I was twenty. I had never mentioned it to Alf during my Under-23 days with him but, like some fairy godmother, he waved the magic wand by picking me for the full international match against Yugoslavia in Belgrade. It was on 9 May 1965 – three days before my twentieth birthday.

Although I had been chosen for the squad I never expected to be in the team. But after a training session a few days before the match Alf took me to one side and said: 'I'm going to throw you in at the deep end. You're playing against Yugoslavia. Don't worry about it. If I didn't think you were ready I wouldn't play you, but I know you won't let anyone down.'

He must have sensed what was going through my mind because his next words were: 'I suppose you want to get on the phone to let your family know?' Dead right I did. I couldn't wait to let my father know that I'd lived up to my prediction.

I don't remember a lot about that first game, although I don't think I played very well. My biggest memory of the trip was seeing thousands of troops with fixed bayonets and tanks rolling through the streets of Belgrade.

I had already earned something of a reputation in England as being a little firebrand on the field. When I saw that lot I said: 'Blimey, they've even heard of me over here and are taking no chances.' It caused a bit of a laugh on the team coach. It turned out it was a parade to celebrate the twentieth anniversary of the Yugoslavs' liberation from Germany.

That match was to be the first of the seventy-two caps I have won for England up until the time of writing (you never know, there may be more to come) and the start of a fantastic run for me under Alf's guidance.

I've worked with some of the top men in the game but there is no doubt in my mind who is the Number One – Alf, by a mile.

He was brilliant tactically, but that was not his biggest asset. His loyalty took the prize. I think that's what got him the sack in the end. He was so loyal to the players who

50

had done so much for him that, perhaps, in the end he tried to hold on to them too long. But could anyone really blame him? They had done so much together.

The scapegoat

No player could ask for more from a manager than Alf gave. The most important thing was that he always provided players with an 'out'. By that I mean that if anything went wrong he was always ready to take the blame.

Players the world over are the same if they've had a bad match. It's never their fault. They have a standard list of excuses to put forward as they sit in the dressing-room.

'The referee was useless ... the pitch was diabolical ... it was too hot, too cold, too wet, too windy ... the crowd was against me ... the other team was only interested in defending ... the ball was too soft or too small.'

Players need outlets like this. If they were too honest with themselves and constantly took the blame every time something went wrong they wouldn't stay in the game long. Their confidence would be in shreds.

But Ramsey provided his players with even more protection than those corny old excuses. If a player had a bad match it was Alf who provided the excuses by taking the blame himself and telling the Press that he had used the player wrongly or that his tactics were at fault.

I know that one of the biggest criticisms of Ramsey's reign as England manager was that he never knew how to handle the Press. He would never put himself out to get them on his side. But I know that he often shunned the Press because he was worried what he might say if he really let himself go. He thought they should be as proud of the England team as he was and that they had no right to knock the side and tell the world what they thought of it. The rest of the world should judge for themselves, in Alf's opinion.

His pride in England and English football was another side of Ramsey's character that made me feel so close to him. He thought everyone should be happy just to wear a white shirt. Money should never be the motive. I think that most of the players went along with him, but one of the few occasions I saw him really upset with his team was over a cash transaction.

We were playing West Germany in Hanover and, as usual, the representatives of the big German sportswear firms, Adidas and Puma, were around pestering players to wear their boots and offering plenty of money as incentive.

I'd had a contract with Adidas for some time and was happy with the boots I already possessed. But now they wanted us to wear new, brighter boots that were more easily identified on television. I refused, it's the biggest crime a player can commit. Breaking in new boots in a match, never mind an international, is unheard of.

But some of the players went into the game with their new boots on. Alf was visibly distressed that any of his team should jeopardise England's chances for the sake of extra money.

He made it clear that he thought the players concerned had let him down. I'm sure that throughout his whole spell as England manager, money was the last thing on his mind.

But he'd get anything else for his team. Only the best facilities were good enough for Alf. I recall a trip we made to Canada for their Expo '67 international tournament. When we arrived at the pitch on which the games would be played we discovered that it had previously been used by a circus and had not been cleaned up.

Now Alf has a strange sense of humour, he's at his

funniest when he doesn't intend to be. He took one look at the pitch and said in his poshest accent, to the Canadian in charge of the tournament: 'It's covered with elephant shit and horse shit. My team can't play on that. If it's not re-turfed we are going home.'

We were all in fits of laughter but the Canadian was amazed. He couldn't believe that the mild-mannered Alf Ramsey could be so outspoken. But they re-turfed it.

It was not often that Alf made such outbursts but when he did he meant every word of it and didn't care about the repercussions. He didn't like the Scots, because he felt that they didn't like the English for no apparent reason except that we were English. And he didn't like the Argentinians – his 'animal' outburst during the World Cup in 1966 proved that. But I don't think he disliked anyone else.

I know what he did like. Cowboy pictures. Naturally, a footballer's life can be very boring at times. When you are away for a match with only training to break the monotony there are not many outlets for amusement. Much of our spare time is spent at the cinema. And if Alf had anything to say in the choice of film, and he usually did, we knew what we were in for – a cowboy.

He loved the guns, the shooting and the blood and the way they talked.

I think the only other thing he loved doing as much was taking part in the five-a-side practice matches with the team. I've never known a manager so keen to kick a ball.

The final great asset Alf had, in my opinion, was that he never left a player out of his squad without telling him exactly why he had done it. He dropped me a few times and substituted me once – and as everyone knows I don't take kindly to such things. Yet I never once resented the axe under Alf.

I always learnt something from what he said and he always left me feeling that the only thing he was interested in was making me a better player.

I know there were some players who have since let it be known that they didn't like playing under Alf. I think you will find that's because they didn't play very often and were not really good enough.

I know of no player who was with him regularly who has a bad word to say about him. That is the real measure of Alf Ramsey's worth to English football. Under him we won the World Cup and could easily have won it again. Since his departure our football at international level has been in a right mess.

He should not have been sacked when he was and I am convinced that had he remained in charge England would still be one of the top Soccer nations in the world.

I will deal with his successor in a later chapter, but for now I would like to take you through the three World Cups in which Alf Ramsey led us and in which I was so proud to take part. At the end I hope many of his critics might agree with me that he was harshly treated by the country he had worked so hard to make great.

Ready to die

Alf Ramsey's opening talk when the England party assembled at Lilleshall for the start of the 1966 World Cup campaign was simple and much to the point.

All he said was: 'I believe I've got the players to win this World Cup and we will win it if we apply ourselves in the right manner.'

He said it with such sincerity and conviction that there was not a player among the forty of us present who didn't agree with him all the way. He had earned our respect and loyalty and he knew that every player in that squad was ready to die for him in the battle that awaited us in the summer of '66.

I was still only twenty-one and playing for Blackpool. I had only a handful of England games behind me but I fancied myself to be among the twenty-two players who would make up the final World Cup squad. I could see from the practice games we played at Lilleshall the way Alf's mind was working.

But it was still a relief when he announced that squad and I found my name among them. I looked at the faces of those who had been left out and felt very sad for them. It's murder to be so near and yet so far, to want to be there and give everything you've got in England's cause.

I think they all accepted Alf's decision. But when you look back there were some fine players among those who were left out, players like Peter Thompson of Liverpool, for example. What England could have done with a player of his ability over the past two seasons!

As the weeks went by and the World Cup grew nearer I started to sense the feeling of national pride growing in the country. It was the sort of atmosphere we had in Jubilee Week. Suddenly everyone felt good to be English. I have never hidden my pride in my nationality, I wish more people were the same all the time.

It was certainly present that summer and all the players knew how much the country expected of us. But we had no fears that the task would be too big. In the games preceding the tournament and in our many practice sessions we had built up a perfect understanding with each other.

I could find Geoff Hurst with a pass in the dark, we had worked on moves so often together. In the case of Roger Hunt, our other man up front, I just used to look for his backside – it wasn't difficult to find.

Perhaps there have been teams with more flair and sheer football ability put out by England over the years, but I doubt if we've ever had a team that was so well equipped to win that particular tournament.

Ramsey knew exactly what we were all capable of doing and never expected any of us to do anything more than that. It was too late for tactical talks now, we already knew all the tactics we needed back to front. Now it was a time for inner strength and outward calm. Ramsey was great at providing the first and making sure that we appeared to have the second ingredient.

While everyone else was buzzing around and getting all excited about the forthcoming attraction, Alf was keeping us occupied with all sorts of diversions – anything to stop us getting uptight. A visit to Pinewood Studios was one of his ideas during the World Cup itself. It did the trick. I was so busy staring at people I'd only seen on film before, I forgot all about the fact that I was in the middle of the most important competition in my life.

During the whole of the World Cup build-up and throughout the tournament I shared a room with Nobby Stiles at Hendon Hall Hotel. It was Room 1 up in the attic. They probably put us up there because we were the smallest and fittest.

I'm not sure why we were paired together, I think Alf just allocated it that way, but for a youngster like myself it was perfect. I couldn't have had a better room-mate.

Nobby might have looked a little villain on the field but off it he is one of the nicest chaps you could meet. He was a bundle of fun off the field and his attitude was typical of the rest of the team.

Every night before we turned in he'd say to me: 'Don't worry, me old mate, we're going to win this Cup. You'll be a hero when it's all over.'

But Nobby was not so confident that he didn't need a few superstitions to help him through. Whenever it was match day he'd wear the same gear he had worn on the day of the first match. Same suit, same shirt, tie, underpants, socks and shoes.

Nobby was really short-sighted without his spectacles. In fact at one England function he left the table to go to the toilet and didn't return for about thirty minutes.

When he did come back, I asked: 'Where the hell have you been?'

Nobby started to laugh and said: 'Well I left my glasses here and when I came out of the toilet I returned into what I thought was this room.

'I've been there all this time and only just discovered I was in someone's wedding reception.'

During that eight weeks Nobby and I really got close to each other, as did the whole team. Nicknames spread very quickly. Banks became 'Fernandel' because he looked like the French film star, Martin Peters was known as 'The Duke of Kent' and Roger Hunt the 'White Hunter'.

The men in Room 1 were just 'Nobby' and 'Ballie'. And by the time the first match came around Stiles' confidence in our ultimate success had completely enveloped me. I played in the opening game against Uruguay, but was left out against Mexico, when Terry Paine replaced me, and against France, when Ian Callaghan played. But I was back for the Argentine game.

Off goes Rattin

I have only two really vivid memories of the Argentine match and the semi-final with Portugal. As the game with the Argentine went on, with neither side seeming able to score, I thought to myself: 'Well, I know there's no way they are going to get a goal, so if we don't this game will go on for ever.' And I honestly think it would have if their captain and central defender, Rattin, had not been sent off. When he started walking to the dressing-room, and I have no doubt the referee made the right decision, I knew we had crossed another bridge on the way to the main objective.

The Argentinians were a well-organised side in defence

but they really never seemed to be interested in scoring. It was an attitude I could never understand.

Neither could I understand why players like Rattin and Albrecht had to go around compulsively kicking everyone.

They were such good players they could have given any team in the world trouble if they'd just concentrated on playing football. They were the one team who, with the right attitude, could have stopped us winning the competition.

The semi-final against Portugal was a classic match to play in and, so I am told, to watch. But from my position out in the middle I never felt there was any doubt about us winning it. The Portuguese allowed us to play and gave Bobby Charlton so much room in the middle.

He revelled in it, and his two goals in that match underlined the fact that we had so much all-round strength. The Portuguese were so worried about Hurst and Hunt they forgot that Charlton, Peters and myself were all capable of knocking a goal in.

But although I knew we had it in the bag that night I still remember praying for the whistle to go to signal the end. The final was beckoning, the last hurdle was in sight.

And, of course, it's that final which obviously stands out most in the minds of all of us, those watching and playing. I remember waiting for Alf to announce the team to play against West Germany and thinking: 'Please God, make him pick me.'

Then he said, as calmly as ever: 'The team that played against Portugal will start the match against West Germany.'

'That'll do me,' I thought. 'Once I've started there's no way I'm not going to finish.'

On the night before the match at Hendon Hall it was again business as usual. No fuss or excitement. Alf made sure we all had tickets for our families, then asked if any of us needed 'sleepers' to help us relax and get a good night's sleep. Before we went to bed, he said quietly, 'It's going to be the biggest day of your lives and you are going to win. Goodnight gentlemen.'

58

My prayer

As I walked on to the pitch at Wembley stadium on 30 July 1966 I think I felt calmer and more alert than I ever have. Normally it's all a kind of blur until the match starts.

But my dad had told me on the telephone the day before: 'There is not likely to be another day in your whole life quite like this one son. Don't let any moment of it pass you by.' And I didn't.

I remember looking around Wembley, seeing all the Union Jacks and thinking, 'The whole world is watching us today. They'll find out what we are made of.'

I felt so proud I thought I would burst. My biggest fear beforehand was that my good fortune wouldn't last. I thought: 'It's a fair bet that someone is going to have a bad game' and I actually prayed that it wouldn't be me – even though I am not a religious person in any sense of the word.

But when that whistle blew for the start I knew it wouldn't be me. I felt terrific. And even when West Germany got that late equaliser that forced us into extra-time my confidence never wavered. And neither had Alf's.

'You've beaten them once, now go out and bloody beat them again,' was all he said. I think some of the players were feeling a bit shattered by it all but there was me, the youngest of them all, thinking to myself: 'I've got to keep

59

running harder than ever to set them an example.' Typical of me, I suppose.

What about that controversial goal that the Germans have been arguing about ever since? All I know is that I probably had a better view of it than anyone else in the ground. I had run out of play so that I wouldn't be offside when Geoff Hurst shot, so I was exactly in line with the West German goal. But I still couldn't say to this day whether it actually crossed the line or not.

The linesman was only yards away from me and I stood next to him when the referee came over and asked him for his opinion. He said one word 'Gol' (sic) and that was it. I went tearing over to jump on Geoff.

But it wasn't until the fourth goal went in that I really believed it was all over. I was running parallel with Hurst and screaming for him to give me the ball. If he had, I had only the keeper to beat.

I suddenly realised that he wasn't going to give it to me, he was going through on his own. 'You stupid bastard,' I shouted and then he hit it, Whack! The ball screamed in and this time I was all over him, calling him much nicer things.

I ran downfield shouting over and over 'We've done it, we've done it.' And it was big Jack Charlton who came to meet me. I jumped into his arms. 'We've done it, Jack,' I yelled again. 'We have and all, cocker,' he replied and I started crying.

I don't think I ever actually touched the World Cup. I swapped shirts with Nobby Stiles instead of with a German as we had agreed to do right from the start and after that all I wanted to do was to get off the field and get in the bath. I later gave my medal to my mother. I thought she deserved it as much as I did.

After it was all over Alf Ramsey finished the affair as simply as he had started it. 'It is your day, enjoy it. I'm proud of you all,' he said. And his parting words to me will always live in my memory. 'Young man,' he said, gripping my arm, 'you will never play a better game of football in your life than you did today.' I started crying again.

I knew Alf was as emotionally shattered as any of us in

that dressing-room but he never allowed it to show. He was still only concerned in keeping things running smoothly.

It was right at the death that the only sour note of the whole World Cup crept in. There was a reception for the players at the Royal Garden Hotel, but for some reason the FA decided that wives and girlfriends of players were not to be invited.

Yet they were the people we really wanted to share our night of triumph with, not the officials who all wanted to shake hands and bask in the glory.

So after a token appearance I slipped away and went to find Lesley who was then still my girlfriend. I don't think I was the only one. After all, the players had been away from their loved ones for eight weeks – and after a day like we'd had, the bedroom was far more inviting than the bar.

The perfect balance

Our build-up for the 1970 World Cup in Mexico had been even more thorough than four years earlier. We were arriving as reigning champions and we knew everyone would be out to get us.

There was the altitude problem, but we had games in Colombia and Ecuador and a six-week spell in Mexico to become acclimatised.

And I think the team we put into action in that tournament was probably the best I have ever played with. It is no criticism of any of the 1966 lads who didn't go into battle a second time. I just felt that the longer Alf was in charge the more solid our game became.

With Francis Lee up front and Alan Mullery reinforcing the middle I thought the balance of the side was perfect. I thought we had a great chance to win the tournament again and I know Ramsey was equally confident.

Our first match was a good work-out against a useful Rumanian side who gave us an early indication of the pressures we were facing. They made no secret of the fact that they would kick us out of the competition if they had to. But we were old campaigners now and not easily intimidated. A 1–0 win, with Geoff Hurst finishing in 1970 where he'd left off in '66, with a goal, was good enough for us.

Then came the match with Brazil. We didn't have to beat them to qualify for the quarter-finals but obviously it wouldn't do us any harm to do so. It was a fabulous match and I thought at the time, and have no reason to change my mind on reflection, that we could so easily have won it.

They had two real chances, the one from which Jairzihno scored their goal and the header from Pele which produced the save from Banks that people have described as the greatest ever.

But we also created chances and the least we could have expected was a draw. But a 1–0 defeat, under the circumstances, was no real problem. We won a hard-fought match with Czechoslovakia and duly took our place in the last eight.

We were paired with West Germany, our deadly rivals who were still convinced they'd been robbed at Wembley four years earlier. There was no doubt in my mind that we would prove our superiority again. And once we had eliminated them I could see no-one except Brazil standing in our way to a second World Cup triumph.

The Brazilians rely very much on their own morale. If they feel confident, they'll murder you. If they start getting jittery, you are in with a great chance. I was getting the feeling that the thought of playing us again was worrying them. Pele made it known publicly that England was the only team they feared. If we beat the West Germans it

would heighten that fear and we could nail Brazil this
time.

Black Sunday

That was the feeling of the whole England camp as we
went into the West German match at Leon on 25 November 1970 – a day that was to become Black Sunday for
English football.

But it all started out so well. Alan Mullery put us ahead,
Martin Peters made it 2–0 and it was all over bar the
shouting. We were really cruising along. I was on the right,
Bobby Charlton in the middle and Martin Peters on the
left. We were controlling the midfield so well that my
opposite number, Wolfgang Overath, never had a kick.

You get that feeling in your gut when you know you
have a team on the run. Overath looked a beaten man,
Germany played like a beaten team.

Then Ramsey made the move that has been argued
about by critics ever since. It is the one thing his detractors
constantly bring up when they try to justify their argument
that he was not a great manager. He pulled off Charlton
and Peters and sent on Norman Hunter and Colin Bell.

Was it the biggest 'clanger' of his career? Did it cost us
the World Cup? My feelings remain now the same as they
did that hot day, a day that I remember vividly as one of
the saddest of my life.

I remember thinking as Hunter and Bell came on, 'Well

done, Alf. That's exactly what I'd have done.' And I'd have done it for the same reasons.

Remember, despite our acclimatisation, it was still hard work playing in Mexico at that height and in that heat. We were all tired, even I who can run for ever. I could see that Bobby Charlton and Peters were both struggling a bit. I'm not saying they wouldn't have lasted the distance, of course they would. But if we did get through – and it was odds-on we would, because no-one had ever come back from being two-down to win against any Ramsey team – they would be needed in the semi-final a couple of days later.

It was tactically shrewd to give them a breather and send on Hunter and Bell who were both strong as lions and ready to run themselves into the ground for England.

What neither Alf on the bench nor me in the middle could foresee, however, was the tactical switch the Germans would make once Charlton was off. They had, for some reason, decided that Bobby was such a threat as a goal-scorer, even from the deep position he was occupying, that while he was out there Franz Beckenbauer was commissioned to close-mark him and do nothing else.

Once Bobby went Beckenbauer was released and encouraged from the bench to start moving forward. And it was Beckenbauer who turned the tide for Germany with a goal. He hit his shot from well out and I suppose Peter Bonetti, substituting for the sick Gordon Banks, must take some of the blame although he might have been unsighted.

It still didn't seem too much of a disaster, we were still a goal up. But then came one of the flukiest goals I've ever seen as a cross-ball hit Owe Seeler on the back of the head and went in. He knew nothing about it. And so there we were going into yet another extra time battle with the West Germans.

Although Alf gave us the same advice as he had at Wembley, somehow I sensed this was not going to be our day. Now it was Overath looking at me and thinking: 'We've got you.'

And they had. Brian Labone was ball-watching when a cross came over, failed to follow the man and Gert Müller gave the West Germans victory.

SYNDICATION INTERNATIONAL LIMITED

SYNDICATION INTERNATIONAL LIMITED

top: Training for Sir Alf and England. *bottom:* The agony and the glory – Haller of West Germany and Alan battle it out in the World Cup Final of 1966.

SYNDICATION INTERNATIONAL LIMITED

SYNDICATION INTERNATIONAL LIMITED

top: England's heroes – the 1966 World Cup Winners, from left to right, (standing) Jack Charlton, Gordon Banks, Roger Hunt, Bobby Moore, Geoff Hurst, George Cohen, Bobby Charlton, (front) Alan Ball, Martin Peters, Ray Wilson. *bottom:* World Cup 1970 – Bobby Charlton, 9, pushes a short pass through to Alan against Rumania. England 1 – 0.

SYNDICATION INTERNATIONAL LIMITED

SYNDICATION INTERNATIONAL LIMITED

top: Sent off against Poland in 1973, Alan sits between Sir Alf and Harold Shepherdson. *bottom:* England's fireball.

SYNDICATION INTERNATIONAL LIMITED

SYNDICATION INTERNATIONAL LIMITED

top: Don Revie and Alan. *bottom:* A welcome to Everton, manager Harry Catterick greets new boy Alan.

SYNDICATION INTERNATIONAL LIMITED

top: The professional foul that succeeded – Alan pushes the ball into the net for Everton against Arsenal. The goalkeeper is Bob Wilson. *bottom:* Everton team-mates surround Alan after their triumph over Chelsea in the Charity Shield Match of 1970.

SYNDICATION INTERNATIONAL LIMITED

SYNDICATION INTERNATIONAL LIMITED

top: Alan rises above Dave Webb of Chelsea. *bottom:* Alan wins his appeal against a booking received when playing for Everton against Liverpool, whose manager Bill Shankly, (right) gave evidence on his behalf.

SYNDICATION INTERNATIONAL LIMITED

SYNDICATION INTERNATIONAL LIMITED

top: Arsenal manager Bertie Mee signs Alan from Everton for a record fee.
bottom: Alan celebrates as an Arsenal player with a great goal against Norwich.

SYNDICATION INTERNATIONAL LIMITED

SYNDICATION INTERNATIONAL LIMITED

SYNDICATION INTERNATIONAL LIMITED

top: A tussle with Liverpool's Ian Callaghan. *bottom left:* Come on Southampton – Alan exhorts his latest club. *bottom right:* The promotion battle at Southampton.

We all sat in the dressing-rooms with our heads down. We all looked back on the game and wondered what had gone wrong. But I can honestly say that not one of us thought that the substitutions had caused our downfall. It was the Press who first put that theory forward and it has grown from there.

I can only reiterate that if I had been in charge that day I would have done the same thing. I will never subscribe to the theory that, at the time, it was the wrong move to make.

I don't think Ramsey was aware of the storm that was to follow. He was obviously as sick as any of us after the match. But he still came around, trying to lift us. He shook hands with us all and thanked us for our efforts. He told us: 'Most of you are all still young enough to be back there fighting in the 1974 World Cup. This time it will be harder because we have to qualify. That's all we must concentrate on now.'

Next day we had the long coach drive from Leon back to Mexico City. All we wanted to do was drown our sorrows and we had some crates of beer loaded up to help us.Halfway back Alf noticed that rugged full-back Tommy Wright sitting at the back of the coach … crying.

Alf went to console him. 'Don't get so upset Tommy. I know we lost but it's not the end of the world,' he said.

'I'm not crying because we lost,' answered Tommy. 'It's just that all the beer has gone.'

We needed a few light-hearted moments like that to help us face the return home to a nation we knew was as heart-broken as we were.

We honestly felt we were very unlucky not to be arriving home with that Jules Rimet Trophy still in our possession. And we were convinced that under Alf Ramsey we would soon find our way back on to that road of invincibility and would be one of the favourites when the World Cup was held in West Germany four years later.

Sent off!

On paper England were not given too difficult a task to qualify for the 1974 World Cup finals. We were in a group of three teams with Wales and Poland.

All we had to do was finish top of that table and we obviously had to fancy our chances. We knew all about Wales and could reckon on beating them twice. Poland were an unknown quantity but there was no reason to expect from their past performances that they would provide any real headaches.

By the time the first match came around, against Wales at Cardiff in November, 1972, there had been a slow but sure change in the 'old brigade'. Of the team that played in the 1966 World Cup final only Bobby Moore, Martin Peters and myself were left. Of the 1970 squad there were Colin Bell, Norman Hunter and Allan Clarke.

We started well enough, winning that Cardiff match 1–0 but I already had the feeling that the present squad did not have the all-round strength of either the '66 or '70 squads. The new boys were leaning heavily on the older players whereas it was time the older players should have been able to lean on the new boys a bit.

The first sign that it was not going to be as easy as it looked came two months later when Wales held us to a 1–1 draw at Wembley. Centre-half Roy McFarland tried to work the offside trap almost on the half-way line. It didn't work and Leighton James was left clear to set up an easy goal for John Toshack. And we only got a draw because of a lucky Norman Hunter shot from thirty yards that could have gone anywhere but finished in the back of the net.

We were disappointed with our performance that night but still felt that we only had to draw in Poland to make certain of qualifying. If we'd achieved that we would need only a draw against Poland at Wembley.

We played Poland at Katowici in June, 1973. It was not a night I care to recall too often. We ran them off the park for most of the first half but on one of their few attacks they took the lead – a goal which was later to cause arguments in our dressing-room between goalkeeper Peter Shilton and myself.

Poland got a free-kick wide on the left. Shilton wanted a three-man wall but I insisted on marking a man. Only a week earlier in Prague we had given away a goal to Czechoslovakia from a similar situation because we'd left a man unmarked.

So I didn't go into the wall. Gadocha took the free-kick and bent it past our two-man wall and it hit Bobby Moore and went in.

Two minutes after half-time Bobby Moore lost the ball on the edge of our box and Lubanski made it 2–0.

And if that wasn't a bad enough night for me already, I was then sent off. Polish defender Cmikiewicz had a kick at Martin Peters' face as he lay on the floor. I saw red, dived in and pinned the Pole to the floor by his throat. I didn't hit him, I just held him there, but the next thing I knew I was given my marching orders.

The arguments went on all night after that defeat. Shilton and I argued about the first goal, others either defended or criticised my actions for getting sent off and the Press were already building up their hate campaign against Ramsey who said after the match that he thought we played well.

From my point of view, the biggest disaster was that I was automatically barred from the return match with Poland at Wembley, although I would have missed it anyhow because I had broken my leg by the time the match came around the following October.

The end for Alf

Alf, generous as ever, invited me to sit on the bench to watch that match. We now needed to beat the Poles to qualify and I took my place next to Bobby Moore, who had been left out of the team, convinced that we would be celebrating victory ninety minutes later.

But well before half-time I turned to Moore and said, 'We're not going to win, Bobby.' I have never seen such an unbelievable match. The closest to it that I can remember was when I played for Everton against the Greek team Panathniakos in the European Cup and we drew 1–1 after hitting them with everything.

The 1–1 draw Poland got that night at Wembley was equally unbelievable. Was Ramsey to blame? I don't think so. Perhaps different players would have had better luck, but you can't pick teams like that. As I say, the squad was certainly one of the weakest Ramsey had put out in a World Cup, but that was because all his best players were no longer available and the replacements were not of such high quality.

All Ramsey could say in the dressing-room after the Poland disaster was: 'You couldn't have given anything more, lads. The gods were against you.' Yet again he was giving them their 'out'.

And I think he knew then that his days were over as England team manager. Isn't it an amazing game when a coat of paint or a flying boot can lose a man his job? It needed only one of the barrage of shots that hit the bar or were saved by the Polish goalkeeper Brian Clough had called a clown, to go in and put England through to keep Ramsey in power.

Instead the country went into mourning, the Press clamoured for his head and by the following summer he was gone.

In my view the Press had sacked a true Knight. He was a hero when the Queen made him Sir Alf and he will always be a hero in my eyes. But if the football public of England were happy the night he went, little did they know what was waiting for them under the next régime.

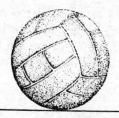

Call from Revie

The first contact I ever had with Don Revie was a mysterious telephone call. I was still at Blackpool and was about to play in the World Cup for England. I wasn't unhappy about playing at Blackpool, but I did think that as an established England international I was worth more money than they were paying me.

I was in dispute over the new contract they had offered but might easily have given in if I hadn't received the phone call. The first call I had came from a stranger who asked if I was interested in speaking to Don Revie. I knew of Revie by reputation for, although Leeds were not then the power they were to become in the next ten years, it was already obvious to most of us in the game that things were beginning to buzz at Elland Road.

I saw no reason not to speak to him and the next call I received was from Revie himself. He told me that he wanted me at Leeds. 'With Bremner, Giles and yourself in the same side we'll be unbeatable,' he told me.

He then suggested that the best way for him to get me was for me to continue my dispute with Blackpool for so long that in the end they'd be glad to sell me – then he would move in. 'Make yourself a real rebel,' he told me.

I pointed out that the longer I refused to sign a new contract the more money it would cost me. 'I'll be out of pocket at least £100 a week,' I told him. 'I can't afford to do that too long.'

Revie's reply really staggered me. 'Don't worry about the money. We'll pay you that for as long as it takes to get you,' he said.

And that's what happened. I used to drive into the moors on the other side of Manchester and Revie drove from Leeds to meet me. He paid me £100 in cash on each occasion and there were at least three of them. 'I need you badly in my team,' he'd say.

But in the end he lost me because his board refused to increase their offer for me by £10,000. As I explained in an earlier chapter my final move from Blackpool came very suddenly when Everton moved in with a £110,000 offer. Before accepting I phoned Revie and told him what was happening, as I felt obliged to do.

It was then that he told me that he had already offered £100,000 which was the highest his directors were prepared to go. 'But give me time Alan and I'll get the rest from them.'

But I was not prepared to wait any longer. I was happy with Everton's terms and felt they were the club for me.

I have often thought about the moral aspects of that episode in my life and, despite the revelations that have since been made about Revie, I can't be hypocritical enough to say that he was wrong to do what he did.

I'm sure I'm not the only player who has been paid in that way. Many managers will do anything to get the man they think will bring their team success and they'll go to any lengths to get a youngster to sign for them rather than a rival team.

If I was a manager I might be tempted to do the same thing. It's all part of the cut-throat side of the Soccer business.

And was I wrong to accept the money and play along with Revie's plans? Again I don't think so. I was a young player with fame behind me but a lot of ambition and drive to go even higher.

If Blackpool had offered me the terms I wanted I would have stayed, I had no other quarrel with them. But if Revie wanted me and it was going to cost me money to help him, it seemed only fair that he should reimburse me. Again I see that as part of the business side of football.

A player's talents on the field are only valuable to him for a very limited period in his life. Is it immoral of him to want to get the best possible profit during that time?

I had no qualms about taking the money at the time and I've lost no sleep about it since. The fact that I didn't sign for him in the end was not my fault. Leeds had their chance and that's what Revie had paid to get.

Revie has never mentioned the incident since. I once read in an article he wrote that he actually cried on the night I signed for Everton. I don't know if that was because he hadn't got me or if he was regretting paying out £300 for nothing.

I think he was right in his judgment. I would have fitted well into the Leeds set-up. They had the sort of players and the motivation that would have suited me. Whether I would have fitted in with Revie's ideas at club level I'll never know, I certainly didn't in international football.

The money obsession

When Don Revie was appointed England manager in the summer of 1974 I was still recovering from a broken leg. So I was delighted to be included in the talk-in he held in Manchester to which he invited the 124 players he considered might figure in his future plans.

I was looking forward to it because, by now, the Leeds success had become a football legend and I was eager to discover just what it was that had made this man Revie so successful. I have always been insatiable in my thirst for football knowledge. I'll lap up any new idea that I think will help myself or my team improve. I was convinced that I must learn something new from Revie.

What a let-down! All I discovered was that he seemed to be still as obsessed with money as he was the last time we had met.

After eight years of playing for England under Alf Ramsey I was very conscious of one thing. No matter how much I needed money to keep up the life-style to which I had now become accustomed there was no way in which I needed any cash incentive to get me to play any better for England.

I may be a bit old fashioned in my outlook but I am still passionately patriotic. I don't know too much about politics, and economics is definitely not one of my strong subjects. But I have this gut feeling that what is really wrong with Britain today is the cynical attitude that seems

72

to prevail suggesting that anything patriotic is a waste of time.

Under Alf Ramsey we were all aware that every minute of every match in which we wore a white shirt we were ENGLAND, that soccer was OUR game and that all that mattered was that we should WIN. And I didn't need Ramsey to instil that feeling into me – it was there from a very early age.

But Revie seemed to fail to recognise this motivation. He acted as though he thought that every extra quid he could make for the players would ensure that they tried just that bid harder.

I'm not saying that Revie was wrong to try and get the best possible wages for England players. As the top men in their profession they obviously deserve to be paid well, just as the best surgeons, lawyers, tailors or bricklayers do.

When we won the World Cup in 1966 we picked up about £460 each after tax. That was a trivial amount even in those days. So I wasn't against Revie trying to raise the international match fee from £60 to £200. What did upset me was the fact that he seemed to think that was all that was necessary. It takes more than that to win World Cups, as Mr Revie was to find out to his cost.

Revie had many good qualities. He was a thorough man, no detail was left to chance in his pre-match build-up. Training and travel arrangements, hotel accommodation and food were meticulously planned. He was – and this may come as a surprise to many in view of what has happened since – a very puritanical man in his outlook.

He frowned on anyone he thought was playing fast and loose when they were away from home, not just players but members of the Press or anyone else he happened to know. And once he suggested that it might help if we prayed every night before we went to bed to ask God to help us become better players.

I couldn't help having a little chuckle over that one, not because I never pray. It was the thought of Norman Hunter on his knees asking for divine help and forgiveness that got me going.

And there were, of course, Revie's dossiers on the

73

opposition. They really were a masterpiece in planning. The only thing wrong with them was that they never worked. He insisted that the players read a dossier in bed – after saying their prayers, I assume. We even had a dossier on Cyprus for the match at Wembley. How ridiculous can you get.

Now I'm all for good planning and good tactical talks before any match. I agree you should know the strengths and weaknesses of the opposition, that your team should go on to the field with a basic concept of how they are going to play and with a set pattern of dead-ball moves. But Revie seemed to think that you could work it all out on a computer and that's what would happen when you got on the field.

His dossiers were all about where No 2 would move when No 3 went somewhere else. No 5 and No 6 would play in one sector and when No 8 went forward No 4 would move to a certain position.

The robots

Revie's dossiers must rank as the most boring bedtime reading of all time, and what's more, it was complete nonsense. It puts fear into players and it should be obvious that you can't play football that way. I'm sure Revie never got his success at Leeds like that. He may have had the dossiers but I bet players like Bremner and Giles took no notice of them – and they were the men who made Leeds tick.

I reckon ninety per cent of goals come as the result of mistakes and having players who are imaginative enough and good enough to make use of them. As I say, you can work to a basic formula, like 4–3–3 or 4–2–4, but you need players with inherent skill and an instinctive ability to see where and when to put the ball.

Revie's methods, I believe, would have produced a team of robots. He bombed out men who tried to think for themselves or looked like being the least bit rebellious. That's why the players who could have brought Revie the success he so much desired were, ironically, the men he rejected.

And what's more he showed another side of his character in doing it – a stubborn streak which, in the end, had to be self-destructive.

He got rid of players in such a way that he left himself no choice if he ever wanted to bring them back again. No matter how badly he might need them in the future, his dogmatic dismissal of them had put them out for all time, the only exception to this I know of being Emlyn Hughes.

The players England needed to take us back to the top were at his disposal, despite his claims when he quit that he never thought he could succeed from the start because he quickly realised that there were not enough world-class players in England.

I agree that perhaps we don't have the same brilliant individuals that were around when England were the greatest in the world. No Finneys and Matthewses, no Carters and Lawtons, no Greaveses, Charltons or Moores.

But if you look at our record in Europe at club level, where we consistently win or come close to winning all the major trophies, how could Revie honestly say we have no players. We have them, but they're not the sort Revie could handle.

Players like Malcolm Macdonald, Alan Hudson, Tony Currie, Charlie George and myself. I'm not boasting when I include my own name in the list of men, I know I was good enough to have stayed in Revie's squad – and, I think, he knew it as well.

But we were not the sort of men who would happily play bingo for hours on end or spend all afternoon on the putting green. We wouldn't take the dossiers seriously, we became annoyed at repeating dead-ball moves twenty times because someone was too thick to understand it the first time.

We just wanted to get on with the job of making England great again – in the arena where it mattered. And we would have done it. But Revie was frightened of us. Above all else he had to have men he knew he could control in all situations. He had to have players who were afraid of him or would follow blindly if he held up the carrot of cash in front of them.

I got into trouble for describing the squad he finally settled on as a bunch of donkeys. I later apologised for using that word, but only because it didn't apply to all of them personally. I still think the analogy was apt. Without realising it the players in his squad were becoming the

76

robots he was looking for. But now I think they realise it was we so-called rebels who were right.

All the loyalty he had demanded from them was shoved right down their throats when he walked out on the job. He had turned on them previously when he stopped using the dossiers and said the players were too stupid to know how to use them.

He blamed the Press for constantly criticising him, the public for not supporting him – he blamed everyone except himself. But he must accept all the responsibility because he didn't do the job he had set out to do – and he didn't do it because HE was the one who made the mistakes. No-one else.

And yet, when I look back, it had all started out so full of promise and, it brought to me some of the proudest moments in my life. To captain England was, for me, one of the highest honours any man can aspire to. Revie gave me that honour and I would have died rather than abuse it. I'd have run myself into the ground for Revie the way I had for Ramsey.

Instead I was discarded after six matches. Revie broke my heart and, I am convinced, eventually cut his own throat for reasons that he has never explained.

Hope and glory

Don Revie's first game as manager of England was against Czechoslovakia in a European Championship match at Wembley. At that time everyone honestly believed that he was ready to lead England into a marvellous new era of attacking football that would sweep us back to the heights.

He had certainly done a marvellous PRO job on the football public. There were 90,000 at Wembley and Revie had put out the message that he wanted them to sing 'Land of Hope and Glory' and to adopt it as our new theme song.

I was in the squad for that match but didn't get into the team or earn a place on the substitute's bench. Yet I felt happy that night because I could feel a new upsurge of English pride. The crowd was marvellous. They sang as if they meant every word and, despite a few early jitters, Revie's new team gave them a 3–0 win to go home celebrating. Things were looking good.

I was substitute for the next couple of games and then we had the match at Wembley versus West Germany. It was labelled as a friendly, but as everyone both in England and Germany knows, there's no such thing as friendly rivalry between our two countries on a football field.

They still had a couple of the players who were in that 1966 World Cup final and they still had the same manager, Helmut Schoen. I was desperately hoping to get my first game under Revie in this match. It would make me the only English player to survive the nine-year gap between the two games.

Not only did Revie grant me that wish, he gave me the biggest present I've ever had. He called me aside at training one day and said: 'Alan, I want you to captain the side against Germany.'

For a moment I was stunned. I had dreamed of this moment for as long as I could remember, but now that it had happened it took a long time for it to sink in.

As usual Revie did a perfect job of getting the best publicity out of the move. He called a Press conference to break the news.

'Over the moon' is an over-used football phrase but there was never a more apt description of my feelings that day. I felt as if I was walking on air. The little lad from Farnworth had finally hit the jackpot. I knew how proud my dad and all the family must be feeling and I knew I had made the right choice all those years ago when I put football in front of everything else.

All the sacrifices I had made as a lad were worth it for that one supreme moment of joy as Revie said, 'Gentlemen, meet Alan Ball, the new captain of England.'

During that Press conference Revie was asked, 'Is this a permanent appointment? Will Ball still be captain if we make it to the 1978 World Cup final?'

Revie answered, 'That's entirely up to him. I am confident he can do a good job for me.'

That suited me fine. There's nothing I like better than a challenge and if Revie was ready to test my ability to lead on the field I knew there was no chance of me not coming through that test successfully. I had captained Everton and Arsenal, two of the best clubs in England, I had played sixty-six times for England and I was feeling more confident than ever about the future.

I still had my doubts about the new Revie régime tactically, but I reckoned that once we found a settled side that would sort itself out. I figured that Revie's secret was obviously in working with a closely-knit unit as he had at Leeds. Until now he had been struggling to sort out all the

79

players in England available to him, but once he'd done that the Leeds magic would start showing itself.

And after that West Germany match I felt more convinced than ever that we were really on our way. Again the atmosphere at Wembley was magical on that night of 12 March 1975. Again I walked out of the tunnel with my head held high opposite our old foe Franz Beckenbauer, the West German skipper.

And I thought we played magnificently. I think it was as good a side as England had produced since the 1970 World Cup finals. It was: Clemence (Liverpool) Whitworth (Leicester) Gillard (QPR) Bell (Manchester City) Watson (Sunderland) Todd (Derby) Ball (Arsenal) Macdonald (Newcastle) Channon (Southampton) Hudson (Stoke) Keegan (Liverpool).

We beat the Germans 2–0 with Hudson having a magnificent match and everyone in the team responding to my demands without question. I loved every second of it. That's always been my strength, urging people on, making them do things they didn't think they were capable of and, I like to think, setting them an example worth following.

There were those who tried to dismiss our performance because they reckoned the Germans were only experimenting and were not really bothered about winning. Rubbish! We were also still experimenting and anyone who has played against Helmut Schoen and his team as often as I have knows that they always care about winning – especially against us.

But we were not worried about any criticism that night. Revie was like a lad with a new toy and I felt drunk with happiness. I also had a few celebration jars that added to that euphoria. The Press raved about the 'start of a new era', they raved about Hudson and they were very complimentary about my leadership.

That pleased Revie almost as much as it pleased me because he had taken some stick about the appointment and I was grateful to him for having defended me. There were even questions in Parliament about it, an MP named Walter Johnson from South Derby stating that it was a 'bloody disgrace' that a player with my disciplinary record should now hold the exalted post of England captain.

But no-one was talking about a 'bloody disgrace' now. We were all heroes again. And I suspect that Revie has looked back on that night many times since and wished he could turn the clock back. If he had kept that squad together, moulded it and perhaps modified it slightly over the next two years, he would never have left himself in a position where the Press and fans, who adored us then, were forced to turn against him for constant failure and he, in turn, was forced to resign for his inability to cope with that criticism.

Instead that side was to stay together for only five more games.

We beat Cyprus 5–0 at home, with Macdonald scoring all five goals, and 1–0 away. We drew 0–0 in Belfast, drew with Wales 2–2 at Wembley and then we played Scotland at Wembley. That match rates alongside all the great games I have played in for England in my estimation.

Beating Scotland has always been important to me. It's equivalent to beating Liverpool when you play for Everton. The Scots love to hate us and they pick on certain of our players to have a go at. It used to be Bobby Moore when he was skipper, it was my turn that day. But as I've said before, the fact that they hated me means, in my philosophy, that they really respected me. And I think I gave them plenty of fuel to keep their fires of hate burning for a long time that day. We didn't just beat them, we destroyed them 5–1.

As Revie and his team left Wembley that afternoon with the English cheers ringing in our ears and, for a change, the Scots silent and demoralised, little did anyone of us anticipate that this would be the last time I would play for England under Revie.

Dear Alan ...

After the Scotland game the season was over and I went off for my summer break well pleased with life. There was a three-day get-together for the England squad at West Park Lodge in Hertfordshire for which all of us gave up our spare time to attend.

I had no hint of what was in store when the first international of the following season against Switzerland arrived in September, 1975. The first I knew of my dismissal was a phone call from a newspaper reporter. It was at seven-thirty in the morning and Lesley answered the phone. The reporter, from a London evening newspaper, offered her £25 for her comments on the fact that I had been dropped. She was completely baffled. She knew nothing about it and neither did I. In fact, I was still asleep. She woke me to tell me what the reporter had said and when the post arrived there was the letter confirming the news (see page 83).

There was no signature on the letter, just Revie's name typed at the bottom and a 'p.p.' from his secretary. The fact that Revie hadn't signed it was doubly heartbreaking.

I honestly couldn't believe that I had been axed. I could think of no reason why I should have been. I was convinced there must have been some mistake. That Revie would get in touch with me personally and explain what was wrong and give me the chance to put it all right.

But the Switzerland game went by, and then the vital

European championship match with Czechoslovakia which we lost and were thus eliminated from the competition, and still not another word from him. And he hasn't said a word to me since.

That unsigned letter holds a place of dishonour in my home to this day – a constant reminder that in this game there are very few people you can really trust.

16 LANCASTER GATE, LONDON, W2 3LW

Our Ref: DR/jc 2078   *Your Ref:*   19th August, 1975

A. Ball Esq.,
9 Whitehall Close,
Nazeing,
Essex.

Dear Alan,

    I hope you receive this letter before you read the morning papers, as I would like to thank you for all you have done for The Football Association and me personally over the last season.

    I have not selected you for the Squad for the Swtizerland match, and I will be making Gerry Francis captain. I have not discarded you completely, and I only hope that you will, if recalled for any special match, play for me. I know this must come as a terrible blow, but I am letting you know first the complete position.

    I hope that you soon get all your difficulties sorted out. If I can help you in any way I will only be too pleased to do so as you know.

    Good luck in the future.

Yours sincerely

J.H Clarke

Team Manager
Dictated by Mr. Revie
signed in his absence

I don't know if the failure to sign the letter was a deliberate way of giving the final twist to the knife, but it certainly had that effect. Did he not have the courage to face me with the news that I was no longer needed or was there another reason behind it all?

These were the questions that kept running through my mind. I was in a state of constant confusion. There was torment, anger, disappointment, resentment all bombarding my brain at the same time.

Naturally, my pride was hurt. I had cherished that England captaincy, but I could have lived with being replaced as skipper if he thought someone else was better equipped for the job.

I was still convinced that I was as good as any midfield player he had available, my legs will be the first to tell me when I can't do a job any more. I could have understood it if Revie had told me personally that he was building for the future and thought he should find someone to replace me immediately rather than wait too long.

But to be discarded after seventy-two internationals with just that lousy letter! That's what got me banging my fist into walls with frustration, and what led me on a campaign of verbal attacks against Revie that made regular headlines.

And my resentment was not helped by the fact that it became increasingly obvious that Revie had not found anyone to replace me, that England were sliding into deeper and deeper trouble. I knew I could help them out of it, but Revie had not just axed me – he'd done it in such a way that he gave himself no room to manoeuvre.

To call me back would have been like begging for mercy. If I was the last midfield player left in England he couldn't do it. He had built his own gallows.

Stories started to circulate around football people and Fleet Street about why Revie had given me the elbow. No-one really believed it was because he thought I was over the top. Only a few short months earlier he had been quoted as saying: 'Alan Ball is doing a marvellous job for me,' and 'I sincerely hope he is still with me when we get to the Argentine.' So what had happened in the summer after our victory against Scotland?

84

Was it the curfew?

I was left to conjecture over my sacking like everyone else in view of the fact that Revie had never confronted me with any allegations. The first rumour I heard suggested that it was connected with a day out at Ascot I'd had with Alan Hudson, who had also been dropped from the England team at the same time and was obviously never going to get back again.

It was alleged that some highly-placed gentleman in racing had been unhappy about our behaviour and had complained to the Football Association. That's nonsense.

Hudson and I did have a couple of days at Ascot. I love horse-racing and I love relaxing with friends at race meetings. It's true we spent a lot of time in the champagne bar, but so did a lot of the Lords, Ladies and Gentlemen who frequent Ascot. After all, we were on holiday and were as entitled to have a good time as the thousands of other people who go there. It had nothing to do with our football and certainly nothing to do with Revie.

The next story that came to me via the back door, that is the sports writers who were closest to Revie, might have been much nearer the mark. It concerned that three-day get-together at West Park Lodge.

I will reiterate that we were officially on holiday and had gone as a personal favour to Revie – but we were glad to do anything we thought would help our future plans both as individuals and as a team.

85

One night, as skipper, I asked Revie if it was all right if the lads went out for the evening, there was not a lot to do at West Park and few of us could stand any more games of bingo – even Ramsey's cowboy films were paradise compared with that.

He said we could, but he warned me that it was my responsibility to make sure that everyone behaved themselves and that we were back by midnight. Unfortunately we failed to beat the curfew. We'd only been into town for a few drinks, nothing riotous, but you know how time seems to slip away when you're having fun.

Anyhow, Revie found out we were late back. Although I was not the last to return he obviously reckoned it was my fault. I did hear later that a taxi-driver who had collected Revie a few days later told him we had to be helped back to the hotel. Revie asked me about it and I told him that in fact we had come back in a friend's car. But he appeared to have accepted the taxi-driver's word instead of mine, although he said nothing at the time.

I accept the responsibility for not obeying his wishes, but I cannot accept that his reactions to it were reasonable or sensible. If he had called me in next morning, laid the law down, warned me that he would stand no further nonsense in the future, I'd have stood for it and made sure there was no repeat. I had played for Alf Ramsey for eight years – and there was no stricter disciplinarian than Alf – without getting into any bother. Why should Revie assume I would change now?

But he said nothing to make me believe that he had decided, on the strength of that incident, that my international career was over. At the end of the week he had a few words of advice for us all and said he wanted us to work on our faults through the summer.

All he said to me was: 'As for you, Alan, your faults and your strengths are yourself.' I don't know what I was supposed to work on from that, but I certainly didn't work on the theory that I was out, finito, kaput.

How many men in this country would expect to have their future dreams torn up and thrown in the dustbin for one night out? We'd all have to turn it in.

Hudson and I were also accused of going to the home of my friend, comedian Bernie Winters, who lived only minutes away from West Park Lodge, for afternoon champagne cocktails.

This appeared, after we'd been dropped, in a newspaper story by one of Revie's favourite reporters and was quoted as one of the examples of our lack of discipline.

Bernie was furious. We had gone there one afternoon when all the others were playing putting or bingo but all we did was have tea and play a few records. So Bernie wrote to Revie telling him that the report in the newspaper was completely untrue. Revie wrote back thanking him for the letter, but it made no difference to our future. He still believed what he wanted to believe, no matter how many witnesses we had to prove otherwise.

Looking back, and accepting the fact that these incidents seemed Revie's only reason for discarding me, I can only feel as sorry for him as I did for myself. I assume the reason he took such drastic action was because, above all, he wanted to demonstrate to everyone that no-one steps out of line with Revie – no matter how big they are.

He himself feared my strength of character. He thought that I would be a constant threat to his leadership and that the players would follow me rather than toe the line under him. He was wrong. He didn't understand me, he didn't realise what that captaincy and playing for England meant to me.

Blundering to disaster

Now Revie has paid for his misjudgment, at least in terms of his reputation, and, I am sorry to say, all the things I said about him and the team during the rest of his reign came true.

I attacked him at every possible opportunity, I was even accused of being unpatriotic – which readers should know by now is the last of my faults – when I went on record as saying I hoped we would lose in Italy.

I did it because, above all, I wanted Revie out. Not merely for revenge but I could see clearly that the longer he stayed in charge the bigger the mess his successor would be left to sort out. Because, once things started to go wrong, Revie completely lost control of the situation. He was like a man blundering about in the dark, walking closer and closer to disaster. His team selections verged on lunacy.

Once he had scrapped the nucleus of that team I captained, he tried to play the same way without having the players to do it. You can play 4–3–3 and win with the right blend. But without myself, Hudson, Macdonald and others whom he didn't like for personal reasons, how could he get that blend?

He picked players who constantly played a particular role with their club and tried to get them to change overnight for England. He had five central-defenders dotted around the team in one match. And against Italy he didn't seem to know what he was doing. He recalled Emlyn Hughes, who like myself had been unceremoniously dumped early on in the Revie era, brought back Stan Bowles and upgraded the untried Trevor Francis. He went to Rome hoping for a draw and finished settling for a 2–0 defeat and calling it a triumph. It was sheer, blind panic.

At the end he said he should have stuck to 4–4–2 throughout, never worried about entertaining football, and just made us an almost impossible team to beat. That's the sort of team we had under Alf – that's what they sacked Alf for producing. No, Revie just didn't have the guts to admit, even on his international deathbed, that he had blundered by sacking the players with talent and hoping the robots would come good.

I normally find it impossible to hold grudges, even against people who have really upset me. But I cannot forgive Revie, not for what he did to me and the way that he did it, but for what he did to English football.

Four years had been wasted. A new man had to start again from scratch and the world was starting to laugh at our feeble attempts to catch up at international level.

No-one has the right to laugh at England and, as the man whom I consider is solely responsible for giving them that opportunity, Revie stands condemned in my eyes as the biggest walking disaster we've ever had, whatever he proves to be for the Arabs.

I have no comment to make on anything else that has subsequently been said about his activities. That is for those who have knowledge of it. I have spoken honestly of my part in his career and I am prepared to be judged on my actions and opinions, and I am prepared to face any man and defend them.

I am willing to tolerate almost anything of a winner. But those who gamble and fail get little sympathy. It's all about winning – I'll go to my grave shouting that.

PART III

What I think

A manager for England

When the Football Association first started looking for the man to replace Don Revie as England team manager I was convinced that they need look no further than Jack Charlton.

I felt he had all the qualities needed to put together the pieces Revie had left scattered behind him and to build an England team that would be as successful as the one he and I had played with in 1966.

I certainly know that Jack would have snatched their hands off had they offered him the job. But when the months went by and no approach came he knew he had been overlooked.

So instead he did a typically Charlton thing – he looked for the toughest challenge he could find. Instead of England's soccer supremo he became manager of Sheffield Wednesday.

He could have stayed at Middlesbrough and plodded along with a team that he had taken as far as he could. But that would be too simple for Jack.

At Wednesday he has a potentially great club that has somehow lost its way. I'm sure he'll get them back where they belong given time.

And the Football Association, obviously not knowing which way to turn for the best, finished up by giving just about everyone else except my candidate a job.

The new set-up under Ron Greenwood is intriguing to

say the least. I will not even attempt to try and analyse the qualities of each of the men involved – and they all have obvious qualities as well as a few weaknesses.

The big question is how will they all fit in to this master plan? Will it be a question of ten heads being ten times better than one, or will too many cooks make a right stew of it all again?

I have never played under any of the men involved, although I have always had a great admiration for Ron Greenwood as a tactician.

At the time of writing all I can say is that I am prepared to be optimistic. I want England to succeed and, therefore, I am, just like any supporter, ready to believe anyone who thinks they can do the job – up until the time it becomes obvious they can't.

I am sure Greenwood knows the problems facing us better than most and that's half the battle. If he can get the rest of his team working with him instead of for themselves he might just do it.

Coaches – and dabblers

British football is not only in the doldrums at the top end of the scale – the international level – we're also in trouble at the bottom. There is an acute shortage of young footballers about who are learning how to play the game properly.

It's not their fault. Schoolboys are just as keen as ever on football and they want to be successful. However, the coaching they are getting is all wrong. There are too many non-professionals dabbling in the game, too many schoolmasters who think they know everything about Soccer but, in fact, are useless.

They go to the shrine called Lilleshall for between two weeks and a month, get an FA badge, and come away thinking they are experts. All they really do is talk a lot and teach little.

I know what happens on these coaching courses because I went on one – and failed. I failed because I refused to learn, parrot-fashion, from the textbooks, written by amateurs, and then spew it all back out again for the people who hand out the badges. That's not coaching.

I think it is impossible for anyone who has not played the game at top level to become a good coach. You can read books until you know them by heart, but you still won't be able to get through to schoolkids what football is all about if you have never known the thrill of walking out at Wembley, or the feel of a crunching tackle.

When I took the course at Bolton all the other candidates, except my Blackpool team-mate Ray Parry, were amateurs. Needless to say they sailed through the exams. Some test that is.

A written paper comes first with all that textbook rubbish. Then they put them in charge of half-a-dozen kids, who know they are on show and go through their paces perfectly and make the coaches look good. Next it's the personal proficiency test, and anyone who can head a ball a few times and go through a few simple exercises can do that. And that's it. There was also a paper on refereeing. Get through that and you've got a badge and are qualified to go out and actually earn money coaching.

It's the sickest joke in British Soccer and the only reason they are allowed to get away with it is that those who influence professional football are too lazy. They don't pay enough attention to this vital part of the game.

Not enough players are interested in going into the coaching side of the business. The new breed of manager is the PRO type who can impress the hierarchy with his bright ideas for making money. And the result is that all the young players coming through are mass-produced – like cans of peas.

They have no more chance of becoming world-class footballers than I have of becoming an astronaut and until we change the system we will never become the world's leading soccer nation again.

I've seen a bunch of lads being coached by some Smart Alec badge-holder. I've watched them shuffling about while he's talking, picking their noses, doing anything except look interested.

Give me that same bunch of lads for five minutes and I'd have them eating out of my hand, listening to every word. Because I know what it's like to sit through boring coaching sessions.

Professional footballers spend ninety per cent of their working lives on the training pitch and if you haven't got a coach who makes that training interesting and entertaining it's murder. I love training and I'll go on for ever with the right man.

There are some who make me feel warm all over. It can be the coldest day of the year but I won't need a sweater because I can feel myself glowing as they talk. They have a passion for the game and it transmits itself to the players. But the others leave you cold. They have nothing to offer that is new, they're mouthing phrases that might just as well be in a foreign language. If the people who are learning have no respect for the people who are teaching them the whole thing is a charade.

I love the chance to coach youngsters. In my spare time I help lads who have got their own team together, like the boys from Harlow called Parndon FC. Great lads who were eager to learn. But schools very rarely ask a professional player to help. I do it for nothing, but instead they get qualified coaches who expect payment and they usually go about it all the wrong way.

I'd show them the way my dad taught me. I would not tell them how to kick a ball, head a ball or pass a ball. Kids are imaginative and you've got to let them use that imagination.

What they need telling is to have confidence in their ability, try the unusual, strut around, take on a player and don't cheat or hide. Once you've got them playing and using their natural talent, then you can start teaching the professional side of the game.

I think all football clubs should be allowed to take players from the age of twelve as they do on the Continent. If they train with top players the kids become like them – that's why you suddenly see hundreds of Johann Cruyffs in Holland or Franz Beckenbauers in Germany. All we get is hundreds of Joe Bloggses. They are the products of 'never-wassers' and are therefore 'never-will-bes'.

They are brought up with the concepts of 'play it safe', 'never take a chance', 'play it square' all the time. That's the surest way I know of killing the game, because by the time this lot reaches the top there won't be anyone around willing to pay to watch them.

It's sheer joy these days to see a lad like Liam Brady of Arsenal. Somehow he has managed to slip through the net as a schoolboy, he hasn't been brainwashed. He loves

97

trying out things, doing the unorthodox. OK, so when he started at Arsenal he sometimes used to get himself into bad positions and he had a lot to learn technically about the game.

But that's when a good coach can be useful. He can spot those faults and put them right – but he can never teach him to do what Brady can already do so well. And no coach must ever stop Brady or boys like him from doing that. Never replace magic with work-rate, genius with technicalities. It's a sure road to disaster. They all have to be interwoven into a pattern that breeds success. That is what professionalism is all about. It's what English football must put right immediately.

Trouble, trouble

My disciplinary record on the field during the first thirteen years of my career was, to be honest, not too clever. As that MP who had objected to me becoming England captain had pointed out quite forcibly it was a 'bloody disgrace'.

I wouldn't have gone that far, but I admit I had not exactly been one of soccer's good boys. In recent years, as I have got older and wiser, my record of bookings has shown a drastic improvement. There was a time when I seemed to be booked every week, for ever in front of the disciplinary committee at FA headquarters and sent off more often than I would have liked.

In fact I have been sent off five times in first-class

football and been suspended for a total of seventy days. Most of that came as a result of my habit of failing to agree with referee's decisions, arguing with them too much and being too involved and impetuous.

It started when I was twelve years old in a form match at school. One of the teachers was acting as referee and I started having a go at him about his decisions. 'Don't be so cheeky, young Ball,' he said. 'You can get off the field.'

I was given detention for it the next day. I knew the teacher was quite right to act as he had, but it didn't teach me any lessons. That was mainly because my father and I decided on a deliberate policy of using my temper and passion to its fullest advantage when I began playing in League football.

I remember my father saying to me: 'Alan, you've got to get hold of this First Division and hit it. Let them all know you are about. You've got red hair so you're easy to spot. Become a real little firebrand.'

I think I took him a bit too literally. I was constantly in trouble, but it never worried me. I was playing so well, getting so much early success, that I had the feeling I could do no wrong.

If the only people who didn't seem to like me were the referees, then so what? Who cared about them anyway? That was my attitude.

My first sending off came in June, 1965. It was in an Under-23 international match which made matters even worse.

We were playing against Austria in Vienna. I got upset with a diabolical decision and threw the ball at the referee. After the match Alf Ramsey had a long talk with me and for the first time I started thinking that perhaps my attitude was wrong, perhaps I was not being clever by getting into so much trouble, perhaps it could ruin my career.

Ramsey didn't actually tell me to cool it or else! He just pointed out to me the things I could give a side with my aggressive attitude and also the things I could lose, for both the team and myself, if I didn't get it under control.

I really began to try harder after that to avoid too much

aggravation – but that old red devil kept leaping into action every so often just the same.

Almost three years went by before my next marching order came, and then it was what the doctor ordered. It was while I was at Everton in a home match against Newcastle, and the referee was a Dr Brady. I don't know what sort of doctor he was but I have vivid memories of what sort of referee he was that day.

He disallowed what I considered a certain penalty for us and I told him what I thought of him in a rather strongly-worded sentence which contained adjectives of a rather crude nature, shall we say.

'Don't you call me that again,' he said to me. 'Why not, you are one,' I replied. That was it, I was off again for an early bath.

I must say that it was very brave of him, sending me off in front of the Goodison Park fans who worshipped the ground I walked on at the time.

Harry Catterick even made me captain of Everton in a bid to help me stay out of trouble. He figured that the extra responsibility of being in charge would make me less inclined to go looking for bother. I don't think it helped too much, in fact it probably made things worse. I was not only arguing with the referee every time I was kicked, I was also doing it whenever any of MY players were kicked. I felt as if I had to stand up for them all.

It was during this spell that the funniest experience I've ever known concerning a disciplinary hearing took place – and as usual it concerned that man Bill Shankly.

I had been booked for a tackle on Liverpool's Ian Callaghan by referee Clive Thomas. I didn't think it was a bad tackle and afterwards both Callaghan and Shanks agreed that I'd been unlucky. They both said they would give evidence for me if it was possible for them to get to the hearing.

By the time the hearing arrived I had been transferred to Arsenal, so I didn't expect to hear from them. But, as luck would have it, Liverpool's Chris Lawler was due to appear at the same hearing, so Shankly came to London with him and also brought Callaghan.

Lawler appeared first and was found guilty – which didn't please Shanks too much. Then it was my turn.

For those who have never been in on an FA disciplinary hearing I should explain what happens and I also should add I think it's a very good system. There is a green board, like a Subbuteo table provided with little players, for witnesses to show where on the pitch the various actions took place.

First the linesmen and referee give their versions, coming in one at a time and using the notes taken at the time to give evidence. Then it's the player's turn.

In my case the linesmen and Clive Thomas had their say, but one of the linesmen had his evidence dismissed because he was considered too far away from the scene of the tackle. When I started to give evidence I felt quite confident of my chances.

I was asked if I had any witnesses and called Callaghan first. Ian said he thought it was a fair tackle and I shouldn't have been booked – and I was now 6–4 on to get away with it.

Then I called Bill Shankly. 'Can you describe the incident for us, Mr Shankly?' the chairman asked.

'Yes I can sir,' he replied. 'But before I do I want to say that the referee in Chris Lawler's case was a bloody liar.'

'Yes, Mr Shankly, but we are no longer discussing that case. We are now dealing with Alan Ball, will you kindly confine yourself to that case, please,' said the chairman patiently.

'I will sir,' said Shanks. 'I saw the incident very clearly from my position in the dug-out, and there is no doubt in my mind that it was a fair tackle and definitely did not deserve a booking for Alan Ball.'

Then Clive Thomas asked if he could put a question to Mr Shankly, as he is entitled to do. He said: 'I understand you to say you were sitting in the dug-out at the time of the incident?'

'That's right,' says Shanks.

'Well I have to inform you that one of my linesmen has had his evidence dismissed because he was too far from the incident. Yet he was standing on the touchline in front of the dug-out at the time. How could you possibly see what was happening if he was in front of you?' said Thomas in triumph.

I looked at Shankly wondering what he would say to that. And his answer will always remain imprinted on my mind. It was: 'When I saw the incident developing I stood up and threw the linesman to one side so that I would have a better view.' He kept a perfectly straight face.

The whole room collapsed into laughter. The chairman, the committee, Clive Thomas, linesmen, Callaghan and myself were rolling about. Everyone except Shanks that is – he couldn't see anything funny in it.

When order was restored I reckoned my 6–4 on chance had now become an even money bet. But I got the benefit of the doubt and managed to avoid another suspension that time.

I have already covered my sending off while playing for England in Poland in an earlier chapter. The other two occasions were both during my career with Arsenal.

The first was in October, 1972, at Sheffield United. Their Welsh international, Trevor Hockey, had been kicking me all over the field. For some reason the fans at Bramall Lane, home of Sheffield United, never liked me and their jeering was not helping matters.

I was having a bad game and finally I snapped after another Hockey tackle and had a kick back at him. Typical of my luck. He'd battered me all the game but my one retaliatory flare-up got me sent off.

My last sending off (fingers crossed and touch wood) was at Derby in February, 1975, and I think that was perhaps the most ridiculous of all, and one which sums up what is wrong on the disciplinary side of the game today.

In the very first minute of the match, Derby defender Steve Powell went over the top with a tackle that sent me crashing to the ground.

I had already broken my leg twice and it was that sort of tackle that every player knows is a possible leg-breaker. So I wasn't too happy about it. The referee came over and asked, 'Are you all right?'

It was obvious he was going to take no action against Powell, referees seldom do in the first minute of a match.

'This is when you are weak,' I told the ref. I don't suppose that endeared me towards him.

Ten minutes later Kevin Hector and myself were involved in a tussle and the referee booked me. 'That's typical of referees,' I told him. 'Through your weakness you've allowed this game to get out of hand.'

And once again the dreaded words were spoken: 'I'm that weak, you can go off.'

I'm not saying I've been an angel over the years, but I also feel that not enough referees understand the emotions involved in professional football. Also there is not enough consistency among referees. One week you can swear as much as you like and not get booked and the next week you say one word out of place and you're off.

All referees seem to have their own pet hates. With some it's bad language, others come down on heavy tackles, and there are those who are only interested in technicalities – like the number of steps a goalkeeper takes or players being ten yards away at a free-kick.

Is it any wonder that players become frustrated with them? That's why they all try everything in the first few minutes to see what they can or cannot get away with. Of course, there are some referees we all know well enough and do not need to sound out.

There was a time when I hated to play in any match which Clive Thomas refereed. We just didn't get on with each other and I always felt he was out to get me, perhaps because I had won that decision against him in the Shankly incident.

Suddenly, however, a couple of seasons ago that all altered. Thomas has admitted that he changed his attitude and instead of being the great 'I am in charge, you do as I say' character of old he suddenly became very approachable. He was just as strict as ever but there was now a feeling that at least he understood what we were up against.

There have been very few like that. I always respected Bob Matthewson, but the two I admired most were Jim

103

Finney and Gordon Hill. They both had the same quality, they were never small-minded and trivial. They considered that, like the players, they were there to help the game run smoothly. If you swore at Jim Finney he'd swear back at you and that was that. If you criticised a Gordon Hill decision he'd say, 'You're not playing too well yourself.'

They won the respect of players and I'm willing to bet that if they booked a player or sent him off, then he thoroughly deserved it.

But I remain convinced that most of the time it's the players who are sinned against. We seem to take the blame for everything that goes wrong with football.

All the mass of supporters seem to do is want to fight, run on to the pitch, throw streamers and anything else they can get their hands on, and generally cause trouble. And we get the blame for setting a bad example.

I think we've become a nation of knockers. Everyone wants to pass the buck on to everyone else, and all they want to do is find fault with things.

We are branded as louts if we have a go at each other on the pitch. But how many of the people doing the criticising have ever felt the pain of the tackle from behind or over the top? If someone kicked them, can they be so sure they wouldn't want to fight back?

There are fights in pubs and clubs every night without any money, prestige or pride at stake. Someone has only to look at another person the wrong way and there's a brawl. It's a violent age and I think footballers do well to curb their feelings as much as they do.

It might help a bit if referees were to spend more time with players during pre-season training. Let them see what we are like to each other when we are being pushed to our limits to get fit. Let them see the work we go through to try and achieve success. They might then understand why we react the way we do when we see it all thrown away by a bad penalty decision or a disallowed goal that we know is good.

The message I'm trying to get across is that it's not always OUR fault. Others can be wrong sometimes.

And my advice to younger players is not to try to copy

104

others. Don't think it's clever to be a firebrand and do it for the sake of it. You'll get enough occasions when you feel like whacking someone without inventing them.

You've got to be at your best for ninety minutes and nothing should be allowed to interfere with your concentration. If you've got a temper, like I had and still have to a certain extent, it is a fair bet that without it you wouldn't be the player you are. So it's no good trying to stamp it out overnight.

You've got to work on it, the way you have to work on everything else in this game.

I discovered very early in my career that players will take advantage of any weakness they spot in your make-up. If you are a coward they will bully you. If you are headstrong they will needle you into going too far and getting yourself sent off.

If you are brilliant, not a coward and have the temperament to take all the knocks and not fight back, you are a genius. Only players like John Charles come into that category.

It took time, advice and bitter experience to get me to the stage I have now reached. But I warn all opponents – I still hate anyone trying to take liberties. I'm just more subtle in my retaliation these days.

The hierarchy

I don't think I shall be staying in football when my playing days are over. That may come as a surprise to many of the people who know how much I love the game, but it is because I love it so much that I will probably be forced to look elsewhere for my future living.

Let me explain that statement. I think by now you may have a clearer picture of the type of person I am. Always willing to learn, but hating to be dominated. And above all I hate hypocrisy.

I have no doubt that as a manager or coach I could handle the players, but I must be equally honest with myself and admit that I don't think there is any way I could handle the soccer hierarchy.

They would have to be a very special breed of directors if I was to be able to work with them for any length of time. They would have to love me so much that they accepted what I did without any argument.

The chairman would have to say to me from the start: 'Look Alan, I'm the boss on this side of the fence and I'm in charge of the rest of the directors. But you are the boss on the other side. And what you say goes, with no interference or challenge from me.'

I don't think there are too many of those around. I'm not knocking directors. I think that ninety per cent of them are smashing people who love the game. But they don't

106

really understand it, or how and why it works from the playing side.

They have, in most cases, had power in football handed down to them. They've been brought up so differently to myself and most players, and I always get the feeling that although they'll occasionally have the odd drink with players, basically they tend to look down on us.

So I'm looking for the perfect chairman who's ready to say: 'Here's a three-year contract. Run it your way. If you fail you're out. If you succeed you get another contract on the same terms.'

If I don't come across one of those, what are the options left open to me?

In order to stay in the game I'd have to join the vast majority of managers who live with compromise. They have to compromise with their ideals, with what they know is the right way to do things, in order to get anything done at all.

I couldn't do that. I couldn't sit back and see something being done wrongly because the chairman thinks it should be done that way. I'd have to stand up and tell him. I'd be leaving clubs at the rate of four a season. That's if I could get that many after the first few.

I know that perhaps I'm a bit cynical about this but I've seen and heard too many promises being broken. They tell you that it's your team to do what you like with, but after a couple of months they are making little suggestions. Then they're making big suggestions and after that you might as well be the tea boy.

They tell you there is money available for players, what they don't tell you is that it's only available for the players they want.

I've seen my father go through it all so often. I helped him clear out his desk when he got the sack from Preston while they were enjoying a good season being eighth from the top of the table. We're too much alike perhaps. We can't flatter people and be polite to them just to stay in work. We have to say what we think and often the men in charge don't want to hear that.

This is why so many of the new breed of managers get

there because they know how to handle directors, not because they know anything about football. And I can't afford to hang about and wait for the men who run the game to be proved wrong.

It sickened me to see people like Alan Mullery waiting so long to get a job, to see Bobby Moore quit the game then sit about waiting hopefully for somone to give him a chance.

What in hell's name is it all about? It honestly frightens me and convinces me that I have to look elsewhere.

My ambition

I have, for many years, been working on a plan that would keep me in with football without having to go against my principles.

I would love to run a coaching school as a private enterprise. I would ensure that every father who thought his son showed promise would be given the chance to find out just how good that boy was.

I would ensure that every boy who thought he could make the grade would get the best advice possible and would discover if he was, in fact, good enough.

Those who were good enough would be given an insight into the life of a professional footballer by the best in the business, because I'd make sure that at least three or four top players would be in attendance every week.

The youngsters would be taught good football habits, they could learn early on whether they have the dedication and stamina to go into the game instead of just floating in as they do now.

All they know about is the glamorous side of football and they're convinced by the sort of so-called coaches I've mentioned before that they are good enough to earn a living in it.

They sign as an apprentice for a club and after three years the vast majority find themselves out on their ear with no other training behind them to get a decent job.

Under my system the parents would obviously have to pay for the coaching and advice they received, but in the end it would be a cheap price to pay compared to the heartbreak and loss of self-respect the present system brings.

This is not just a pipe-dream of mine. Together with friends, I have already had talks with Harlow Development Corporation with a view to getting the land and building permission to start such a school there. Backers came forward and the plan expanded to include squash courts, restaurants, swimming pools and what have you.

The latest news on this scheme is very hopeful. I don't give in easily and I'm learning all the time the pitfalls of living in the big world outside football, so that I will walk out of the game as well-prepared as I was when I walked into it.

Moving to Southampton has been a real blessing in that direction. For the first time in my career I am living in a relaxed atmosphere. The pace of life is not so frantic and I can understand why Mike Channon stayed so long and was able to build up a business background that will give him a firm foundation for life when he finishes as a player.

For, although I started right at the top, was twice transferred for record-breaking fees and have always been on top wages, I've never been able to do what Mike has done – build for the future.

Living in places like London and Liverpool as a football star puts you in a bracket of society that forces you to spend money as fast, and sometimes faster, than you earn it.

The time not spent in football is invariably spent enjoying your hard-worn status. There is little time for sitting back and planning ahead.

I'm not complaining about the life and I'll tell you more about it in a later chapter. I'm just explaining why I am not the wealthiest player in the game and why, as I get older and wiser, I become more convinced that footballers are shabbily treated compared with almost every other sport. I read of tennis players and golfers, motor racing stars and jockeys, basketball players and skaters who are all millionaires. I know it only applies to the very best in the sport, but it does not apply to the very best in soccer in this country.

That is why so many of our better players are being forced abroad and why so many youngsters will not even enter the game – they'll get a tennis racquet or a golf club in their hand if they've got any sense.

I'm certainly not going to let my lad, Jimmy, dive into football just so that he can follow in dad's footsteps. I'm going to let him try everything and if he has the aptitude for one of the other more money-making sports I'll do everything in my power to give him the chance to make it.

As I've said, now that I'm living in Southampton I can understand how players in this environment are able to concentrate on a business as well as playing football, but I can never understand how someone like Franny Lee managed to do it while playing in Manchester.

I tried it once when I became involved in a garage business in Cheetham, just outside Manchester, in 1967. It was about as successful as some of my racehorses had been – the worst of them.

I just could never afford the time to get on top of it and, naturally, it lost money, leaving me about £10,000 out of pocket. I've not been alone, most of the players I know have gone into similar ventures and come out poorer than when they started.

Playing football at top level is such a full-time business with constant training and travelling, that I cannot see how it can mix with business enterprises. 'How on earth does Franny Lee sleep at night?' I used to wonder.

But he's made it and good luck to him. For the majority

110

it's stay in the game, if you've got the right temperament or ability, or fall back on the age-old footballers' retreat of a public house.

I don't want to do either and, although I'm a late starter in this neck of the woods, I think the Hampshire air might still have reached me in time to get something sorted out for the future.

Fan-tastic

Although I was a bit critical of the mass of football supporters in an earlier chapter, those hooligans who only get involved in the sport because it gives them a chance to run riot and have a punch-up every Saturday, I must now stress that there is also a vast army of marvellous supporters.

The people who turn up to follow their local clubs through the good, the bad and the indifferent times. Those who live, breathe and eat football. The men, and women, who will travel anywhere to see their team in action. The fanatical, who don't care how foolish they look at times, and the influential, who don't care how much money it costs.

I've met a good cross-section of this amazing group of people, without whom football would not exist, and I could not write this book without mentioning some of them.

After my first game for Everton, which as you remember we won at Fulham and I scored a goal, we went to

111

Euston Station to get back to Liverpool and there I saw this little man standing on the platform.

As we walked towards him he suddenly rushed up to me, threw himself on his knees in front of me and said: 'Alan Ball, God sent you from heaven to Everton just to score goals like that.'

It was an amazing introduction to the fervour of Merseyside support which never ceased to amuse and delight me.

I was walking to the ground one day with a suitcase in each hand. 'Sign your autograph please, Alan,' says this chap pushing his book in front of me.

'I can't, I've got both hands full,' I said.

'That's okay, pal. Just spit in the book then,' he answered. I ask you!

But one of the most fanatical of all the Evertonians was a man called Eddie Cavanagh. Some of you may recall his spectacular run on to the pitch at Wembley during the Cup Final when the chasing policeman lost his helmet to the amusement of 100,000 fans and the wrath of the constabulary.

I didn't condone his action that day, and, at that time, I thought he was just another of the bovver boy brigade. It was later that I met the real Eddie Cavanagh, discovered just what an unbelievable supporter he was and was delighted to become the godfather of his son who was christened, would you believe, Alan Ball Cavanagh.

There were thousands of such characters in Liverpool but I'll never forget Eddie. And there are just as many in Manchester where I spent much of my social life and made many friends.

One of those social evenings landed me in a spot of real trouble one night. I was at Blinkers, a well-known club frequented by many of the Manchester players. I'd had a few drinks and on my way home I was stopped by the police and breathalysed. They decided to press charges, but, like all good friends, one of mine came along when I needed him most.

He was club owner Selwyn Demmy, a nice man and I'm glad to say a very observant one.

He noted that I had finished my last drink just before I left Blinkers at exactly two a.m. When the police breathalysed me it was two-ten a.m. and the law stated that there had to be a clear twenty minutes between the last drink and the time you took the test. It was Selwyn's evidence that got me off the charge and saved me a lot of aggravation. He didn't have to come forward, there are many who would have said: 'Another footballer in trouble, they're all the same,' and left me to it.

When I moved to Arsenal there seemed so many people about me all at once I couldn't take it all in. But I soon sorted out the hangers-on from the genuine article. Those who only wanted to be seen with footballers and those who would go out of their way to help them – and there are times when footballers do need a lot of help and advice.

Such a time is during their testimonial year. It's a very important event for a player who has stayed loyal to one club for ten years and hasn't been able to cash in on the transfer market.

It's their one big chance to get some money behind them, but they need all the assistance they can get in organising testimonial matches, dinners, dances and other fund-raising events. Remember, the player is still involved with playing for ninety per cent of his time and he gets little time for such a big operation.

And it's then that you see the really good guys, the supporters who are prepared to do more than just jump on the glory band-wagon.

I came across many of these in London, helping players like George Armstrong, Frank McLintock, Pat Jennings and Frank Lampard. Such nice blokes as the brothers Jimmy and Pat Quill, who were particular friends of mine, Leslie Wise, Maurice Keston, Archie Davies, Terry Creasey, Johnny Driver, Ernie Felgate, John Brain, Ken Platt and Ron Bowden. My thanks to them all, not just for what they've done for me but for helping all the lads in the game.

And there's another very special man I have to mention, one that many of the fans might have got the wrong idea about over the years.

He's big fat, lovable fella known to the players as 'Fat Stan'. His real name is Stan Flashman and I have a great deal of affection for him.

Stan is one of the biggest ticket salesmen in the business, and I don't just mean his size. He is called, by the people who don't like his business, a ticket tout and whenever there are stories about inflated prices for tickets at Cup Finals it's the men like him who are blamed for it.

They're called black-marketeers and parasites. Those who label Stan in such a way obviously know very little about the man. He's the only person I know in his game who has to go out and get the tickets because he's so inundated with demands for them and just can't bear to let people down. He doesn't snap up as many as he can get, then cast around looking for mug punters daft enough to buy them at inflated prices.

And I can also honestly say that if I ever let Stan have a ticket it will be going to someone I know personally. He just saves me the bother of being hounded, and that goes for all the other players.

Does he make a living off our backs? Not likely, I've even known him lose money to help the players. I was in his office once and saw a whole pile of tickets for Arsenal's third-round Cup-tie with Tranmere. He'd bought them off the players knowing there would be no demand for them but his philosophy was that he couldn't expect to get tickets for a top match if he didn't take them for the less glamorous games as well. To me, that's the sign of an honest man.

And if I've ever done him any favours they've been more than well repaid. My wife and I have seen stars like Frank Sinatra and Sammy Davis Junior with tickets numbered Row A, Seats 12 and 13. They don't come any better than that and he could have got £300 a time for them. Instead he gave them to me.

If that's a parasite he's not too good at it. As far as I'm concerned he's a hard-working man who has got to the top in his particular trade and deserves the rewards like anyone else.

And it hasn't taken me long to make many new friends

114

at Southampton, people like David Dean who made me instantly welcome.

Show-biz

Apart from my friends among the fans – the lifeblood of football – I'm also happy to mix with the stars of other sports and entertainments.

I've enjoyed being in the company of tennis star Jimmy Connors at a party after Ascot at David Frost's, and I've played golf with players like Tommy Horton and Neil Coles. I went to the wedding of another great golfer, Jack Newton, who came so close to winning the British Open.

When I mentioned things like this to friends at one time I always had something of a guilty conscience, I felt as if I was name-dropping. But now I realise that I have every right to be with top names – because I reckon that we footballers are as important as anyone.

I'm not being big-headed, just honest. For too long the footballers of this world have allowed themselves to be treated like servants instead of masters. When I started mixing with show business stars I always felt somehow inferior. Then I realised that they were as happy to meet me as I was to meet them. And I have to admit that I love being in their company.

I met many of them at parties with Mike and Bernie Winters. I became friends with Peter Sellers, Frank Ifield, Lionel Blair and Jimmy Tarbuck.

I went to Ascot with David Frost and Elton John. I was

welcomed at the top night-spots like Tramp where manager Johnny Gold was so good to me. It was just great to relax with people like Marty Feldman and Anne Bancroft.

They are all beautiful people who have reached the top of their profession. They are winners and I deserved to be with them. I think that is what winning is all about – living on equal terms with all the other winners.

It's not some sort of ego-trip. Just a reward for all the hard work you've put in, all the things you've missed to reach the top.

And I also discovered that if you have natural talent you should never let anyone try and kid you that doing it your way is wrong.

I remember a long talk I had with Bruce Forsyth. I asked him how he could act so naturally and be so good with people on television.

'It's just a gift, I do it all off the top of my head,' he told me.

That's what it's all about. Having the confidence to back your own talent. That's why I now refuse to bow to authority just because they have authority. I know I'm right about football and I will never allow anyone again to rob me of my right to declare it.

The greatest

Football fans will always argue about who is the greatest player of all time, the greatest team of all time and that sort of thing. It's great entertainment in pubs and clubs and you can bet your life that no two people will ever entirely agree.

I try and simplify that game by saying, 'I can't argue about the players who went before me because I didn't see them or play with them. But I'll argue with you for ever about the greatest players I have played with or against.'

Because, for a footballer, that is the true test. If you want to know how good a player really is then put him in the other side and you'll soon find out. It's on that premise that I nominate George Best as the greatest in my book – and after all, it is my book.

Most of the people you hear putting forward authoritative views on the subject have never actually walked on to a pitch with the players they're talking about and tried to stop them or beat them.

I think I've come up against all the great players of the last two decades and have walked off the field feeling proud to have shared it with them. There have been so many wonderful players about but if you pin me against the wall and say 'Name your top team' I would have to begin by saying: 'I'll have George Best for starters.'

George Best arrived on the English football scene at about the same time as I did and I have no hesitation in saying that he's the best I've ever come up against. He has everything – unbelievable skill, scores great goals, a complete individual in his style and always a great entertainer.

But, as everyone knows, George found it very difficult to live with the fame that great talent brought him. I knew him as well as most and as we once had shares in a racehorse. I've had many great nights out with him, both in Manchester and London. But knowing him and understanding him are two entirely different things.

It's easy to try and label George as this, that and the other. Too many late nights, too many girls, too much booze. It's not that simple.

It was a combination of all those things, but summed up I think it was that George was 'hooked' on living a full life. He was like an alcoholic, but it wasn't drink he was addicted to, it was life itself. He had so much going for him, but at the same time he had nothing. He was like a wild stallion that everyone admired but no-one could tame. You just couldn't get a rope around his neck.

But, at the root of the whole trouble was the fact that George didn't really have anyone to let down, except himself. I could have been a similar type, but as a young man I had my father as an anchor. I was so scared of doing anything to upset him there was no chance of me taking the wrong road.

After that I had my wife and family to keep me aware of my responsibilities. Best had nothing – and that makes it a sad story for me. I can't go along with the image that was built up of an ungrateful star who couldn't care less.

Yet, despite all the problems he faced at the end of his career at Manchester United, Best has come through it and matured. He played some magical football for Fulham in his return to League football and no matter what he has said or done I can never forget the years at Old Trafford when he played football that no-one has ever matched in my era.

As we have started my team with Best let me continue along the forward line. And next must be Pele, the Brazilian who has stunned the world with his skill for as long as I can remember.

118

There can be no weakness in his football make-up, the man can do everything and a bit more. But, whereas the only problems surrounding Best showed when he came off the field, there were psychological aspects about Pele that showed up on the field and constitute the main reason why I put him second in my list of great forwards.

Pele just could not live with the constant problem of being marked out of the game, or kicked out of the game, which is what usually occurred. I know it should never happen and a player with his talent is entitled to feel upset and become violent himself when it does. But it is a fact of football life that any dirty trick in the book is used to stop players whom the gods have gifted with extraordinary ability.

Best was kicked more than any other player in Football League history, and often finished up as the villain of the piece himself, but it never interfered with his dedication to win and come back looking for more.

Pele did not have that total commitment. When the crunching was obviously not going to stop he would limp away. It is a characteristic that doesn't stop him being great – it just puts him a shade behind Best as far as I am concerned.

And third on the list comes Denis Law – which proves just how good the other two are. Because it was Law who was my idol when I was a young player, the one I tried most to copy.

The thing I admire most about Law was that he changed from being a great midfield player to become a striker and was even better at that. He was impossible to mark tightly and scored goals that took your breath away, particularly with his head.

After I had made my mark in English football during the 1966 World Cup I realised that, from then on, I would be a marked man. I knew that I would have to overcome this if I was to advance any further in the game. It was to Denis Law that I turned for advice on that subject.

I watched film of him in action, noted the way he could put just that fraction of a distance between himself and a defender without anyone really noticing, and how he could

119

sprint from a standing start with such speed that no-one could keep up with him.

I learned enough to help me overcome the close-markers but not quite enough to become as good at it as Law was.

The fourth member of my forward line would be the great Dutch master, Johann Cruyff. The thing I like most about Cruyff is his simplicity. He never over-elaborates but does the easy thing well and, having lulled the defence into feeling safe, he has an electrically quick burst of speed that takes him past people.

He makes great goals and he scores great goals. Again, he is a difficult man to man-mark but, like Pele, he can be put off by a defender who sticks with him and is not stopped from breaking every rule in the book.

But he is well worthy of a place in my forward line – an attack that would make any defence in the world sweat just thinking about it.

With four forwards like that, Best, Pele, Law and Cruyff, it's obvious that I'm going to have a 4–2–4 line-up. So who gets the middle two positions?

My first choice would be the great Brazilian star Gerson. He's the greatest passer of the ball I've ever seen. And his all-round play was out of this world during the Mexico World Cup series.

I spent a long time thinking about the second midfield role but in the end came up with the Italian, Benetti.

He's very strong in the tackle, always aware of what is going on and knows a lot about the game.

I'm sure that Gerson and Benetti would provide the sort of quick, accurate service my front four would need. As a midfield man myself I have very strong views on that role.

I have been playing what has been known as the Continental style for ten years, but I know there are a lot of fans in England who don't really appreciate it. When people praise me for what I have achieved it's always my work-rate they admire.

But I didn't have to study the game or learn very much to achieve a high work-rate – my natural enthusiasm ensured that I'd be covering a lot of ground and always wanting to be in the action. What I had to work on was the art of providing a service for the goal-scorers. The quick one-two with short but deadly accurate passes.

The fans love the men who do the clever running with the ball. The whole world admired the Matthewses and Finneys of the game. They raved about Kevin Keegan. They love players who look exciting and I'm not knocking that. In my forward line I've picked four of the most exciting players you could wish to see.

But the whole art of football is to keep it as simple as possible, do the easy thing well. Without a good service the best forwards in the game can do nothing.

It's the men who provide that service who seldom get the glory. They do their job unnoticed by the majority. It's only the men playing with them who fully appreciate what they are doing.

Men like Ian Callaghan, who I believe should have won more England caps than he did, and Alan Oakes of Manchester City, who didn't win any caps and must be one of the most underrated players of my era. He was so consistent for so many seasons. He'd win the ball and start moves with the long or short pass. He'd tie the middle of the field up for you, and with that achieved, you're more than halfway to winning the game.

There are many about like Oakes who do most of the work but get little of the glory. I saw the new young Dutch player, Jan Peters, in action during a tour of Holland recently. He is a typical example of the top Continental midfield player. There's nothing really showy in his play, but he cuts his mistakes to a minimum. He's a master of the ten yard ball, and in my experience that can cause more trouble than all the forty-five yard passes that can be seen and cut out by a well-organised defence.

Gerson and Benetti put into practice perfectly my ideas of what great midfield players should aim to achieve.

That brings me to the back four. In the centre of that line I have no hesitation in choosing England's Bobby Moore and West Germany's Franz Beckenbauer. They have dominated European and World football as defenders and have constantly proved that you don't have to be just big, hard and destructive to succeed in their position.

121

They have developed the art and technique of defending with brains instead of brawn. They both read the game brilliantly, cut out trouble by shrewd positioning instead of crude tackling, and they can both move forward and start an attack of their own with perfectly placed passes.

I have never seen two players who can stay so cool and calm under pressure. Are they too similar to play together? Knowing them they would soon sort out a system between them that would make a back line virtually impregnable.

I have played with Moore and against Beckenbauer, but I would not like to distinguish between them. I'd be only to happy to have them both.

The full-backs provide no real problems for me. At right back it must be West German Bertie Vogts.

He marked me when we played them in Mexico and I have seldom come against a quicker or tougher tackler. He did a terrific job also on Cruyff in the World Cup final in 1974.

Vogts is a real terrier, who never lets up throughout the whole game and is the sort of competitor every team needs.

And at left back I don't think I've ever seen a better performer than England's Raymond Wilson. He was a joy to watch in action, sharp in the tackle but classical in his style. I saw Ray mark Garrincha, the little Brazilian winger, when he was at his best and I doubt if the 'Little Bird' had ever had his wings clipped so effectively.

So far I have included only two English players in my 'greatest' team, Moore and Wilson, but there has to be a third and I don't think anyone in the world will accuse me of unfair bias when I nominate Gordon Banks as my goalkeeper.

Banksy is one of those 'keepers who finds his best form on the biggest occasion. I know people who have seen him playing perhaps six times a season for Stoke and cannot understand what all the fuss is about. But have they ever seen him play a bad game for England? In fact, have they ever seen him play anything short of a brilliant one?

Banks had everything a world-class 'keeper needs. He knew all the angles, by that I mean he could work out almost exactly where any shot would go if hit from a certain position, he was strong and brave and he had brilliant reflex actions. Can anyone ever forget his save against Pele in the 1966 World Cup?

It's a marvellous feeling to play in a side knowing that Gordon is your last line of defence. There have been other marvellous goalkeepers, and England has seldom had a bad one. But with due deference to them all I cannot place any of them in the same league as Banks.

So that's my team: Banks (England); Vogts (West Germany), Moore (England), Beckenbauer (West Germany), Wilson (England), Gerson (Brazil), Benetti (Italy), Cruyff Holland), Law (Scotland), Pele (Brazil), Best (Northern Ireland).

It makes me feel warm just to think about seeing that lot in the same line-up. As I've already stated there are a million combinations and a million arguments to come out of an exercise like this.

But everyone is entitled to his view and I would under-line that I have actually played with or against every player in that side and that is the only way I consider you can really judge how good a player really is.

The Clan

A business man I know once had the idea of forming a syndicate of some of the better-known figures in football in order to use their names to make money for them all.

The plan was to form a pool of personalities who would be hired out for promotional and publicity purposes, opening shops and fêtes and all the usual activities that give footballers and other stars extra cash perks. It never got off the ground as it happens, but I well remember the initial meeting in a London restaurant. It was a fantastic day out and we were immediately christened 'The Clan'.

The interesting thing about it all was the list of people invited to join this exclusive club: myself, Peter Osgood, Alan Hudson, and Malcolm Allison were among the founder members. Notice anything in common, apart from football, with that group? We are all also members of Soccer's so-called 'bad boy' brigade.

Bad boys, that is, as far as football's establishment is concerned. The fans don't call us that and neither do the companies who are only too happy to use us in their promotional campaigns.

What is it that makes a player a 'bad boy' in the eyes of the soccer bosses? It's not the much-publicised drinking sessions or the newspaper articles or television outbursts. It is simply that those in authority, and managers in particular, just do not know how to handle players who will not conform to their regimented ideas of running a football club.

Players of exceptional talent have complete belief in their own ability and, and a result, they do not need a manager holding their hands for them every day and night. And it is because of this that they cross the thin dividing line that separates the good boy from the bad boy image.

The good boys are those who, for some reason, do not have this absolute faith in their talent, they do not feel strong enough to be masters of their own destiny. If the manager told them to walk backwards they'd do it. They will conform every step of the way.

The 'bad boys' fear no-one, they fear no situation, they fear no institution. Fear is a terrible thing in this game. It turns good players into mediocre players, and average players into bad ones.

Lack of fear and honesty is what gets so many of our most talented players into trouble. Because they know they can play the game and can produce the goods on a Saturday afternoon, they will openly go into a bar for a drink during the week. They cannot understand that there are people about who actually hate them, who feel that because they pay to watch them play they have bought a share in their personal lives.

It is these people who will phone a manager the following day and turn three or four drinks into a drunken orgy. That gets them into trouble.

By the same token, there are people who love you. They will tolerate anything as long as you go out on that pitch and make their hearts sing with delight. These are the people who get you out of trouble. I've never known a breed of people like top footballers who are so constantly in and out of hot water – and I don't mean taking baths.

I know all the controversial characters, and I don't hide the fact that I am one of them, Hudson, Osgood, Stan Bowles, Malcolm Macdonald, Charlie George. I know what the jealous people say when another headline appears: 'There he is again, that flash merchant, shouting his mouth off, letting the manager and the rest of the team down. Who does he think he is?'

I'll tell you what he is. He's just a normal guy who is at the top of his profession and doesn't like being ordered about like a little kid by someone for whom he has no respect.

I've never been ashamed to go out with any of the so-called bad boys, and I'm careful about who I choose as friends. And I am convinced that they can all be handled without any trouble by a manager who knows his job.

I'll admit that being a football manager is one of the hardest jobs in the world – but they get well paid to do it. And players have as much right to expect managers to do their job properly, as managers have the right to expect the players to play at all times to the best of their ability.

As far as I'm concerned one of the most important parts of a manager's job is an awareness that you can't dress a team up in club blazers and expect them all to behave identically and to all react to the same treatment in the same way.

Some need the iron fist, some the soft soap. And there are those who, if they were not extroverts and outgoing characters off the field, would not be the players who do the unexpected and the unusual on the field – the sort of things that win matches for you.

But how do managers treat these individuals? They tell them: 'The rest of the team has done it, you must do it.' That's a sure sign that trouble is on the way, that's why players like Hudson and Macdonald are sent home from tours, that's why I've had rows with managers, that's why Osgood and George have had transfers, that's why Bowles is always in the hot seat.

And what do the managers say to defend their disciplinary decisions? 'No player is bigger than the club.' Rubbish!

The club is made up of people, it doesn't exist without them. What most managers mean when they say that is: 'No player can be seen to be bigger than me.' And that's what is at the root of this whole 'bad boy' syndrome.

I've known of managers who go out and buy a player, knowing exactly what sort of problems he is likely to face, knowing where previous managers have gone wrong in

126

their attempts to control that player. But they still make the same mistakes, they still think it is the player who must change his personality rather than that they adapt their rules to help integrate him. It's nonsense.

Of what use is the player if he changes from someone who fears no-one, including the opposition, to someone who fears the manager and everyone else? Too many managers want to be sergeant-majors. They should try being psychologists instead.

Hudson and Supermac

Alan Hudson has been a very good friend of mine for a long time and I know of few players with so much talent and so many problems.

He has somehow got himself into the situation where he has almost been forced out of the game, branded as the man no-one can handle. What a waste of so much talent.

Yet, Alan is one of the most easy-going people I know. The only thing that upsets him is being pushed around by people whom he considers are completely inferior to him on a football field. It means, unfortunately, that with the current breed of League managers there are few he can work with.

Terry Neill of Arsenal is certainly not one of them. I am convinced that it was a mistake for him to buy Hudson in the first place and I think he did it purely to keep the Arsenal fans quiet when he sold me. I consider there was no real tactical thought behind the buy, it was simply to save his own neck.

Malcolm Macdonald was another Neill signing at Arsenal, but there can be no criticism of that buy. Macdonald was worth the money and was a great capture for Arsenal in my opinion.

I soon discovered that Malcolm has exactly the same attitude about the game as myself. He knows what he can do, he doesn't consider it a crime to say what he thinks and believes, and he is prepared to back his achievements against other peoples' prejudices and opinions.

He's called 'Supermouth' by his critics, he is brash and arrogant, but he produces the goods and he scores the goals. What more do they want? It's the same old theory. If he wasn't so arrogant off the park he would not be a scorer of goals on it. You can't have it all ways.

Peter Osgood, who has now moved to America, had far more than his share of troubles in English football over the years, but again I don't think he deserved half the bad publicity he received.

After joining Southampton I was as close as anyone to Peter. The reader may wonder why, wherever I go, I always team up with the player with the 'bad boy' image.

Birds of a feather, you say. I think not. It's just that I only feel comfortable with those who like to live life, who have something to say for themselves, the characters of this world. I like people who can make me think, those who can make me laugh, those who make me feel warm. I'd even prefer those who make me angry to the aimless, faceless wonders who go through life scared to make an impact, worried about what people think of them, incapable of taking a chance.

Ossie is a character all right, and a hell of nice one. He is also a fantastic footballer, at his best one of the most creative players in Europe. And all he needed was to be appreciated now and again.

All a manager has to do to keep Osgood interested and happy is to pat him on the head and tell him how well he is playing. It shouldn't be difficult, particularly when he is playing well, which is most of the time.

But I'm afraid there are those, and Dave Sexton appears to be one of them, who find it impossible to make that simple human gesture. I have never worked with Sexton so I cannot be too specific, but he has always struck me as a man who tries desperately hard to hide his true emotions. He feels it would be a weakness. If he had rushed up to Ossie after a match and given him a hug no-one would have thought the worse of him, and Ossie would have played his guts out next time.

Instead, at Chelsea, Osgood constantly seemed at war with Sexton, who appeared to think that he was loafing about the field. After almost a year with Osgood I came to the conclusion that he did have a stamina problem, he could not chase all over the field, he did have to wander back downfield slowly after a long run up it. And no amount of abuse or disciplinary action will alter that fact. If you want to make use of the real Osgood talent you have to accept some of the faults as well.

To my knowledge, Lawrie McMenemy never had any complaints about Osgood's behaviour. He knew how to handle him, and so did I. I could get Ossie going without any bother. Just point out little things to him, ask him to try doing something this or that way, make suggestions that might improve his game, and he'll respond. And when he does, praise him.

Perhaps I should take over a team of so-called bad-boys when I quit. It would be an interesting challenge, but I am convinced I could handle them.

I reckon most managers have got their priorities all wrong. It's not the players who refuse to toe the line off the field they should be worried about, it's those who cheat on it – and there are some of those about.

They are always on the edge of the action, always looking busy but never really getting involved. They hide behind players, pull out of tackles and are generally always in bed when the manager says so.

They are the ones I'd bomb out, because they'll never win you anything. No matter what my reputation off the field, I can honestly say that throughout my whole career, and that covers a lot of minutes so far, I have cheated for only forty-five of them.

It was while I was playing for Arsenal in a match with Tottenham. Coach Bobby Campbell ordered me to play wide on the right with Eddie Kelly filling my normal role in the central midfield position.

I was not happy about it, mainly because I felt that it meant he fancied Kelly as a midfield player above me. It depressed me and when I went into the match I couldn't have cared less whether we won or lost and throughout the first half I just wandered about doing nothing in particular.

Campbell realised instantly what was happening, the cheats of the game couldn't fool him for long, and at half-time he said simply: 'Get back into the middle and start playing.' In the second half I ran myself to a standstill.

It did not appease Campbell. After the game he gave me a real roasting in front of the rest of the team. 'Whatever happens, whatever instructions you are given, no matter how badly you feel about something, taking it out on your team-mates during a match is not the way to solve it,' he told me.

And he added: 'By doing that you let everyone down, including yourself. If you have a grievance take it up after the match. You're a professional and you are paid to give a hundred per cent effort at all times.'

He didn't get any arguments from me. I knew from the start that he was dead right and that I was completely out of order. I had never done it before, and I have never done it since. I don't honestly know how some players can do it week after week. Luckily they are in the minority. Most of us are prepared to sweat blood on the field, providing we are allowed to replace that lost liquid afterwards.

Astle's vodkas

It was a question of too much liquid refreshment being consumed at the wrong time – or so people thought – that gave another player a 'bad boy' reputation.

He was Jeff Astle, the West Bromwich Albion striker who was in the England squad during the 1970 Mexico World Cup. I sat next to Astle during a flight from Colombia to Mexico that was to put him into the headlines all over the world.

Jeff was never the best of air passengers, in fact he was one of the worst and needed a drop of 'Dutch courage' to see a flight through at the best of times. This particular flight was anything but that. It was the worst I've ever known.

The weather was diabolical and we were caught up in violent thunderstorms that sent the plane into crazy spins, dropping hundreds of feet at a time without warning and eventually forcing us to make an emergency landing. I could see that Astle's nerve ends were rapidly wearing thin.

I wasn't feeling too good myself, I don't think anyone on that flight had experienced anything quite like it before. Every time the air hostess came by Jeff was ordering another vodka and orange and there was no way I was going to stop him. I realised it was the only way he was going to complete the journey without having a real crack-up.

By the time we reached Mexico City, of course, Jeff was

well gone, and to make it worse the waiting photographers quickly caught on.

Next day the newspapers had big headlines and pictures of the 'drunken English footballer' arriving for the World Cup finals. Alf Ramsey tried to cover up by saying Jeff had been on tablets to calm his nerves and these had caused his illness. But the fact was that Astle was stoned and Alf knew it. He proceeded to give me the biggest rocket I ever received from him.

'You should have told me he was drinking heavily,' Alf told me.

'I couldn't get the lad into trouble, boss,' I replied.

'Are you trying to say you can't trust me, Alan?' he stormed, and I could see he was really upset.

I still don't know who was right. Alf would probably have understood Jeff's problem, and would have tried to calm him down by talking to him. But as far as I was concerned the vodka was the best cure for Jeff that night.

Incidentally Astle was a great revelation to the rest of us on that tour. He has a really dry sense of humour and was a great chap to have around during a tense trip like that.

For me he will go down as making one of the wittiest off-the-cuff remarks of all time, when his club, West Bromwich Albion, signed goalkeeper Jimmy Cumbes from Tranmere for £30,000.

Cumbes was also a fast bowler for Lancashire at the time and when Astle heard about the signing he said: 'Typical of this club. For an extra £10,000 they could have got John Snow.'

Cloughie and Mal

Brian Clough rightly has a tremendous record as a League manager, but I know for certain that I could never play for him.

He is the sort of manager who has to dominate his players, his strength lies in the fact that he surrounds himself with players who will always accept his strictures.

If I joined him he would try to dominate me but, despite his record, I would not have the respect for him to let him do it. I'm convinced that's what went wrong at Leeds.

Cloughie had been too used to having his own way with the players he had bought and controlled at Derby. When he got to Elland Road he came up against the Billy Bremners and Johnny Gileses of this world. And he could not compromise or compete with them.

He couldn't just arrive and slowly analyse the situation, then gradually mould it to his own personality. It had to be 'Clough is here, you'll walk in fear' – and it didn't work at Leeds.

I know his record with Nottingham Forest is almost unsurpassed for success but I must stick to my original opinion, however stubborn that seems.

But, no sour grapes, Clough does what matters – succeeds.

He knows how I feel about him and he has made no secret of the fact that he's not too enamoured with me.

We had quite a chat in Torremolinos when both

Southampton and Nottingham Forest teams were staying in the same hotel. The Southampton players were always relaxed and happy, the Forest boys acted as if they were on the parade ground – none of them would dare put a foot out of line.

From my close-up view of him during that trip I got the impression that Clough was a very arrogant man and during our talk I told him what I thought of him.

I finished by saying: 'There is no way I could ever play for you.'

He replied, 'I might not want you to play for me.'

And, the next day he told our manager Lawrie McMenemy, 'One of your players verbally attacked me last night, you ought to be more strict with them.'

What a statement from a man who made his reputation on verbal attacks. I'm sorry, I know how the fans admire him, but Cloughie is not for me.

I've never worked with Malcolm Allison but I have worked against him – and that is the best way to get to know a man's qualities.

And, as far as I am concerned, big Mal has many great qualities as a football coach. And the greatest of them all is that he could always win when it was most needed. Like so many gifted and talented people he's had his personal problems and made headlines in newspapers that have not always endeared him to the public. That's not my concern. To me, he's a winner.

He's like a great racehorse trainer. If you give him a specific target to aim for, Allison will reach it. He'll make sure his team is ready for the big match – the one that really matters.

Those who don't really know the man, think he's flash, someone who talks a great game but never gets any further than that. I know differently.

I once spent hours talking football with Mal and I have never been so enthralled. He had so many in-depth views about the game and he expressed them so magnificently that I left him convinced that he would reach the top.

I think it's a tragedy that he has been lost – only

temporarily, I hope – to the top grade of English football. The man loves the game and has so much to offer.

When I was about to sign for Arsenal, Mal was then at Manchester City. He rang me at home the night before I actually completed the signing and said: 'Join me, I'll make you the best player in Europe.'

He then asked me what terms I had agreed with Arsenal. When I told him he said, 'Carry on and sign for them, son. There's no way I can compete with that.'

I admired him for his honesty then, and I still do.

The brothers

I know brothers come in all shapes and sizes but I am constantly amazed by the difference between Bobby and Jack Charlton.

Bobby is always the quiet character, you'd hardly know he was there in a crowd. But you would never be in any doubt about Jack's presence at any function.

Bobby was a great, natural player. A great passer of the ball with a brilliant shot in either foot. I always enjoyed playing with Bobby but I must admit it was hard work.

He'd knock forty-yard passes then move for the return and I found myself constantly racing for a ball and having to control it and give it back while he strode majestically into space.

After a few of those runs you knew you'd been in a game. But Bobby did not have the sort of personality that could dominate people and was in many ways just too nice a guy to be a football manager.

Jack is a different type. He had to work hard to become a top player. For many years he lived in the shadow of his brother's genius and was considered a plodder by many critics. But the great thing about plodders is that they always get there in the end – and Jack was as important to the England success in the 1966 World Cup as Bobby.

And it was then that his personality took over. His success with England and Leeds gave him the respect of other players while his strong will ensured that no-one stepped out of line.

I know Jack was criticised when he was at Middlesbrough for producing a so-called dull team. But I don't think he had any alternative.

In order to survive in Division One they had to play to their strengths, and let's face it, how was he going to persuade top, attacking players who could take their pick of any club in Britain, that they should live and play in Middlesbrough?

While on the subject of brothers there is another footballing duo I'd like to comment on. They are the Knowles brothers, Peter and Cyril.

I played against Peter when he was a young inside forward with Wolverhampton Wanderers and was convinced then that he had a great future in the game. An England forward without doubt. So I was surprised and upset when I read that he had chucked the game in to follow the Jehovah Witness religion.

As you know, I am not strong on religion but I have nothing against those who are. Every man has the right to do as he likes with his life. But I couldn't help feeling at the time that Peter could have served his purposes better by staying in the game.

Muhammad Ali now makes the point that the reason he hung on so long as world heavyweight champion was to help the Muslim cause. As the champion, people would listen to him and respect him. Without the title he was just another preacher.

Peter felt he could not condone some of the practices in

the game, particularly the violence. But surely he could have done more to solve that as an insider. Still, I have always followed my convictions and I suppose I have no right to criticise Peter Knowles for doing the same.

But brother Cyril comes into an entirely different category. I have had my share of quarrels with other players, usually in the heat of battle. But I don't think I ever held a grudge against any of them – it's all over once we are off the pitch.

There was one exception – Cyril Knowles, the England and Tottenham full-back. He gave me a gash in my leg that required eight stitches and I never forgave him for it.

It wasn't the injury so much. I've suffered two broken legs and more knocks than I care to count, that's all part of the game. But there was something about the way Knowles went into that tackle, and his attitude after it, that really got me going.

I did something I've never done before or since. I vowed I would get him, sometime, somewhere. But he retired from the game with a bad injury before I could retaliate. Perhaps it was just as well – I'd have probably got into more bother over it.

137

Keegan was right

Kevin Keegan's transfer to SV Hamburg in the summer of 1977 for £500,000 has prompted many people to ask me since: 'If you were twenty-six years old and had received a similar opportunity would you have gone?'

In order to answer I have to get one thing clear. Do they mean would I have gone abroad when I was twenty-six or would I go if I was twenty-six now? Because my decision would be different in each instance.

I would certainly not have left English football when I was twenty-six. There was not a lot to be gained at that time, either financially or in terms of prestige.

But if I was twenty-six now and had the chance Keegan has had I would have to consider it very carefully. And I must admit I would probably have made the same choice as Keegan.

He has to be better off financially, particularly in terms of the current tax situation in England. And he cannot lose out as a player. I think two or three years on the Continent will make him a better player and he can still return to English football at twenty-nine to reap the benefits of his experience.

Keegan is only one of many players I expect to be making the trip across the Channel in the near future and I also think that the future of football will almost certainly involve a league of top European clubs.

There has been talk for many years in England of a

138

Super League, on the lines they have in Scotland at present.

But I think it's too late for that. The idea will be overtaken by a European League with the top clubs from England, Holland, West Germany, Italy, France, Spain and perhaps even the Eastern European countries involved.

As for the rest of the Football League I cannot envisage it continuing in its present form for very much longer.

Clubs cannot afford to travel from Hartlepool to Torquay and Swansea to Darlington on the gates they are now getting. Neither can they afford to keep a staff of full-time professionals.

The only way the majority of Third and Fourth Division clubs can stay alive is with part-time players and regional leagues. It certainly won't mean the end of football as Britain's major sport, just make it a bit more manageable.

PART IV

The other Ball

True blue

I have tried hard to broaden my knowledge of life and not let myself become tied down to football alone. I read a great deal, with Leon Uris as one of my favourite authors.

I am not a religious man, that is to say I am not a practising Christian as such although I rate myself as Church of England for official purposes.

As far as politics go I vote Tory, a fact that may not go down too well in my home town of Farnworth which is mainly a mining community. But I have always figured that once you enter a certain wage-earning bracket you are mad to vote Socialist. It's not an argument or a subject I'm prepared to get too involved with too often, however.

I do want to be more aware of things around me and if ever I find myself getting too far into the clouds and believing that I am above it all, I need only a weekend with my grandfather to bring me right back down to earth with a bump.

That's not my father's dad, Jimmy, who helped me with my football as a lad and is now dead. This is my mother's father, Norman Duckworth, who spent all his life as a miner when the going was really tough – he'd picked coal in an eighteen-inch-high seam, on his knees with his back doubled-up all day.

He's never been abroad, but I reckon he has a few lessons to give to those who think they know everything. I never tire of talking to him.

I remember taking him to a midweek match at Old Trafford once. I can't remember who United were playing but I knew it would be a nice treat for him. I bought the best seats in the old stand there.

During the game it started to rain and, although we were under cover, the rain was being blown into the stand and we were getting soaked.

He always wore a flat hat, I don't think I'd ever seen him without it, and suddenly he took it off and put it into his pocket.

'Why have you done that? It's pouring down,' I said.

'Eh, lad, I can't sit down and watch television tonight with a wet hat on, can I?' he replied.

It's the sort of crazy, but beautiful logic that I love and it's long talks with him that bring me down to earth and stop me losing my sense of proportion.

Sport of Kings – or villains?

Some people think that a sense of proportion means that a footballer should never go near a racecourse. For some reason, which I have never understood, everyone else in the world can go to a racecourse, gamble as much as they like and have a marvellous time and nobody else gives a damn. But if a footballer does it he's either a fool or a villain.

I've lost count of the times I've been accused of being a waster, heard whispers that 'He's skint again, done all his money on the horses.' Or been warned that I'd come to a sticky end associating with those 'no good' racing types. I don't suppose anybody ever said that to the Queen, or the Duke of Norfolk or any of the other noble patrons of the Sport of Kings.

I'll admit I love racing. Apart from football it gives me a bigger thrill than any other sport or form of relaxation I know. But in no way am I a gambling maniac and never have I left myself in a position where I regretted having a bet.

I know a lot of top footballers who feel the same way as I do about the horses. They're prepared to gamble and have a go. They love the thrill, the surge of adrenalin when they're on a winner and even get a smile out of the hard luck stories when they've backed a 'cert' that trails in last.

They go into it with the same zeal with which they enter a football match. It's winner takes all.

Of course, there are a few who go over the top. Stan Bowles has admitted that gambling has been the cause of most of his problems off the field and he's not the only one I know like that. But that's their problem.

It's easily done if you are the sort of person who never discovered the right time to say 'No'. When you are a young, successful footballer, there are always people only too happy to hang around you. They're the natural parasites of this world. You find yourself buying three rounds to their one at the bar and at racetracks you find yourself backing their tips and giving them back-handers when they win. You never get any back when the tips go down.

If you allow that to get out of hand you're in trouble. I learned very quickly in life when to say 'No'. I pick my company carefully and when I go to a racecourse I take my friends – they don't take me. Another rule I learned very quickly is not to have an account for gambling – it's an easy way to do your money in.

It's no good betting unless you are prepared to lose. I go to a meeting with a set amount in my pocket which I can afford to gamble. If I lose it, that's it. I'm not about to start borrowing to chase my losses.

Perhaps, compared to the average punter, I do back heavily at times, but it's all relative to what you earn. The most I've gambled on a single bet was £250. It lost, but I didn't contemplate suicide. The most I've won in a day was £1,000 when I backed three winners. I didn't get carried away and try to do it every day – it's like everything else I've attempted in life, if I start I like to be good at it.

I'm not putting myself forward as a racing expert but I think I know enough not to be a mug-punter. I learn as much as I can about horses from trainers and jockeys and I read the racing 'Bible' – the Sporting Life – from front to back every day. Putting it simply, I just love racing.

But I've never ridden a horse in my life, not even had a donkey ride on the beach. If I had, and had liked it, who knows? I might have become a jockey like the gentlemen

146

who didn't want me at Bolton suggested. They were right about me having the build for it.

I was sixteen, however, before I discovered that racetracks and bookmakers existed. I had just joined Blackpool and went to Haydock Park one afternoon with some of the older players. I didn't have a bet then but I was thrilled by the atmosphere and the excitement.

By the time I got to Everton I'd learned all the ropes and at Goodison I found no shortage of company for my racing excursions.

It was my Scottish international team-mate Alex Young who first introduced me to the joys – and heartbreaks – of being an owner. Between us we bought a two-year-old called Daxel for £1,500. We had it trained by Barry Hills. I was destined to learn the heartaches before any of the joys. To put it politely it was a bad horse. In the end we were lucky to get £400 back on it. But, undaunted, I tried again. This time my partner was George Best and the horse was called Slim Gypsy. This one was trained by Ian Walker but although it was placed a few times it soon became obvious that Alan Ball was part-owner of another bad 'un.

So that was sold, again at a loss, but, brave as a lion, I was soon back in business. A Scots friend and I paid out £1,200 apiece for another two-year-old called Gargon Prince, and would you believe I finally owned a winner.

It won four races as a two-year-old and I really thought I was on to something good. Unfortunately it had flattered to deceive and never won again for us. But at least we broke even on that one.

I'll always remember my first bet as a winning owner. I couldn't get to the course so I backed Gargon Prince in a betting shop at Southgate in North London. I had £80 on it at 13–8 and I think I could be heard all over North London shouting it home inside the final furlong.

By now I'd really got the taste as an owner but the next time I was involved it was only for a one-tenth share in a horse called Go Go Gunner. The ten of us were either Arsenal players or supporters and our racing colours were the red and white of Arsenal. We paid £500 each, so it wasn't a rubbish animal.

I actually went with trainer Ian Walker to Newmarket sales to look for a horse. We decided on 'Gunner' and I helped in the bidding. It was another side of racing that fascinated me.

Lester Piggott's tip

Go Go Gunner ran second in its first two races and really looked a promising animal. Then, towards the back end of the season, it ran at Newmarket and Ian Walker engaged Lester Piggott to ride it. I had a broken leg at the time, but I was not going to miss being in the parade ring on the day Piggott rode our horse.

I had been an admirer of his for many years, he's a real winner – one of the all-time greats in Sport. So there I was, on a miserably wet and windy day at Newmarket, the only owner of the horse in the ring for the last race of the day. As Piggott came into the ring he doffed his cap to me. 'No need for that,' I said 'You're the maestro, I should be doffing my cap to you.'

It was a fantastic feeling to see him in our colours. All he said to me as he mounted was, 'I'll win.'

That was good enough for me. I may have had a broken leg but I broke all records to get to the rails to put on the £100 I'd brought up with me. Again it was 13–8 and Lester was as good as his word. He won by three lengths in the six-furlong race and there was never any danger.

I started shouting the horse home from four furlongs out and felt hoarse myself at the finish. But I had enough chatter left when I went into the unsaddling enclosure. As Piggott dismounted I must have asked him twenty questions in about half a minute. 'How did he handle? Will it win next time? How good do you think it will be? Will it go over a longer distance? ...'

Piggott gave me the most withering look I've ever received in my life and answered simply, 'Nice horse.' That, I am told, is a long sentence for Lester.

The next time I met him was at Chester races. I'd left it late and couldn't get a hotel room but I was very friendly with jockey Geoff Lewis and he let me share his room for the night. The following morning at breakfast Lester Piggott strolled over to our table. 'I'm at York next week,' he said, and walked away again.

I quickly worked out what that meant. I rushed to the telephone to get hold of Ian Walker. 'Lester wants to ride Gunner at York next week,' I told him. Walker said he thought the race our horse was entered in at York was a bit warm for him, but if the maestro wanted to ride it who were we to argue. So Lester was booked.

We all reckoned we were on a certain winner. It started at 6–4 favourite and I had another £100 on it. But there was no repeat celebration. It finished third and this time Lester's advice was: 'Drop him in class next time.' He'd found out just how far the horse would go up the ladder of success and never asked to ride it again.

That's what I admire about the man – a true professional. I never tire of listening to the racing lads tell stories about Lester. One of my favourites concerns the wealthy owner who was travelling in an aeroplane with Piggott from France. Piggott is not the smartest dresser in the world and this owner started taking the mick out of him.

'Why don't you buy some decent shirts with your monogram on like I do?' he asked.

'My shirts may not be as flashy as yours, but I'm not frightened of losing mine,' answered Lester.

We had one more really big win out of Go Go Gunner.

It was at Windsor and this time Pat Eddery rode him. The trainer fancied our chances and I did my usual in-depth analyses from the *Sporting Life* information. The danger was called Moor Lane but I reckoned that was a short runner and might not get the trip. So the syndicate decided to plunge.

We backed it down from 7–1 to 9–2 and I think everyone on the course at Windsor must have been on it. And it duly obliged. Sadly the horse had reached its peak and soon afterwards we sold out. But that won't be my last experience as an owner.

When I left Arsenal and moved to Southampton I found myself teamed up with some real racing enthusiasts, none bigger than Mike Channon who owned some really good horses including Cathy Jane, a top-class filly. Mike, Peter Osgood and myself had some really marvellous days out racing.

Channon is a real character who loves horses even more than I do. He'll have a bet but it's the thrill of the sport that he enjoys most. I thought I could shout a bit but Mike used to drown me. I remember a steeplechase meeting at Newbury when Mike was roaring his fancy home at the second last.

One of the real huntin', shootin' and fishin' types was standing near us and said to his wife: 'There's that Channon chappy. He loves his horses but I wish he wasn't such a noisy bastard.'

That's what I love about racing. You meet all sorts of people and most of them are terrific. If horse racing is a weakness, it's one I'm prepared to live with.

What Lesley thinks of me

I've now told you as much as I know about Alan Ball. How I think, how I feel, what I believe and what has happened to me as accurately as I can recall. But that is like looking into a mirror. I only see the image of myself that I want to see. There are other Alan Balls that even I don't know about.

And there are at least two people, equally as qualified as I am, to portray a picture of the Alan Ball the public has never seen or heard about.

They are my wife and my father. I have talked about the part they played in my life, but what part have I played in theirs? How do I rate as a husband and a son?

It was the Scottish poet Robbie Burns who talked about the gift to 'see ourselves as others see us'. It's a frightening thought, but I've been prepared throughout this book to admit things about myself which I have kept locked away in my own mind for so long, that I might as well go all the way and find out what the 'other' Alan Balls are like.

So here goes. This chapter I will hand over to my wife Lesley and I can assure you they are her words and her thoughts, with no prompting from myself ...

Lesley writes: 'I was only fourteen years old when I first met Alan. I was his sister's best friend and it was only natural that we should get to know each other in such a small community.

I think the first real memory I have is travelling on a bus with his sister to a coffee bar. Alan and his friend, Terry, who has since emigrated to New Zealand, were also on the bus – they'd been to cricket practice.

I was convinced Alan was going to ask me out, but he didn't. I soon discovered that he was very shy with girls. He was the typically aspiring sportsman who thought more about football than anything else.

Eventually he did pluck up the courage to ask me to the pictures and we've been together ever since. But getting Alan to ask me out was, I discovered, only half the battle.

His father's insistence that he stay away from girls was a constant hurdle we had to overcome during our courting days.

But it never really bothered me. Perhaps a lot of girls would have given in, but I found the challenge exciting. There never seemed any doubt in both our minds that we would get married and, if anything, his father's efforts to stop us merely served to cement our relationship.

Of course, I knew from the start that being the wife of a footballer was going to be different from the average marriage. His father had been a footballer and I was already well aware of the problems facing a wife in those circumstances.

I must have been asked the same question thousands of times during the last ten years: What's it like being married to a football star?

I always answer: "It's the same as being married to anyone else." But, to be honest, that is the easy way out.

The truth is that it is the same as being married to anyone who is in the public eye, whether they are sportsmen, show business stars or politicians.

There are extra pressures and anyone who marries a footballer must go into that marriage knowing what to expect.

And the first rule for the wife of any footballer is to learn to be independent. Your husband is away so often, it can be as much as three months at a time during a summer tour, that you must learn to look after yourself and to become a person in your own right.

152

Alan was in Mexico for eight weeks during the 1970 World Cup. In 1976 he spent eleven weeks in South Africa.

I must admit there are times when it gets me down. In the final analysis you have to weigh the advantages against the disadvantages. And always I come up with the same answer. I'd rather be married to Alan than to anyone else who was home on the dot at six o'clock every night.

I suppose you get used to the idea that he is going to be away. In fact, you can become so used to it that when he is home again there is a very awkward period of readjustment.

I become so used to doing things, organising the life of myself and the children in a certain pattern, that Alan must feel like a stranger when he returns after a long trip and I tend to resent it when he tries to change the routine.

And you have to live by a routine when you have three children as we do. It is obvious I miss Alan when he is away but there's no chance of feeling lonely. There are enough problems dealing with the children to keep any wife fully occupied. There's Mandy, she was ten in January, followed by Keeley who was six last December, and finally Jimmy who was two last September.

And, naturally, being the children of a footballer they were all born in different places. Mandy arrived in Liverpool, Keeley in Manchester and little Jimmy was born in Paddington, London – not the station I may add.

I enjoy being a mother and like to think I cope as well as most. The hardest part is that adjustment from Alan not being there for weeks on end to being at home and under your feet every afternoon.

But it's a problem I have overcome and I cannot understand wives who try to influence their husbands' careers to suit their own needs.

I have heard of players who have turned down the chance of going on tour with England or playing in the World Cup because their wives refused to accept such a prolonged absence from home.

I would say there are certain Dos and Don'ts involved

153

for any footballer's wife. The biggest *Don't* is that you never hold him back.

If a wife is not prepared to take the disadvantages she does not deserve the advantages and she should not have married a footballer in the first place.

And the second *Don't* I have learned, particularly with a character like Alan, is that I never, ever, become critical of his performance on the field.

Alan knows only too well if he's played well or badly and he does not want me chipping away at him. He hates me watching him play, and I'm sure the main reason for that is because he doesn't want to hear my comments after the match.

For a start he doesn't think I know enough about the game to have any comments worth making, and secondly he thinks I might be influenced by the people around me at the match. So my visits to football grounds are few and far between. But, in fact, I thoroughly enjoy going to a game – but only if Alan is playing. I wouldn't dream of watching a match in which he wasn't involved.

I become really excited during the game and before it I think I am more tense than Alan is. That's probably another reason he doesn't like me around before a match. My tension could transfer itself to him – and he has the knack of being able to completely shut himself off from all emotional ties once the game has started.

A perfect example of this occurred when our Mandy was a toddler. She slipped and her hand went through the glass window on our front door, severing an artery.

She was rushed to hospital and Alan, who was out at the time, received a phone call telling him to get there immediately.

He had no idea what had happened and was in a real panic when he arrived. The shock had a terrible effect on him and he was like a zombie for the rest of the week. But on Saturday he just snapped out of it as if someone had pressed a button. No-one watching him play that day would have known anything had happened.

That's when his professionalism shows through and that's another *Don't* for a footballer's wife. Never come between your husband and his employers – the football club.

Footballers come into a different category in this respect from even the show-business personalities. In most cases they go into the game straight from school, in fact they are going from one school into another and they are, to a certain extent, still treated like children.

Everything is done for them and by the time they have reached manhood and become married they just accept this way of life. The club and the manager become God to them.

They only see it subjectively, but, in most cases, the wife comes into the scene with a fresh eye and sees it all very objectively.

Because I had almost grown up with Alan, I was aware of these attitudes but there are times when I still become annoyed about decisions made by the club and the manager.

"Why do they stand for it?" I ask myself. "If it was me I'd soon put them in their place."

But if a wife starts that sort of nagging it will do her husband no good at all. The footballer has learned to accept the strange way his bosses sometimes think, and his wife has to curb her natural tendency to argue about it and just has to follow suit.

But when it comes to following her husband blindly the most difficult time of all for a footballer's wife comes with the inevitable transfer. It's difficult enough moving home at the best of times, that is when you're moving because you want to, in order to get a better house or to live in a nicer area.

But to be completely uprooted from your relatives and friends and dumped in a strange part of the country almost overnight is a terrifying experience.

You've just got your home the way you want it, you've made many friends and the children are settled in school. Then crash! Another club moves in with a transfer bid, your husband's club decides to accept and you're off. You can spend weeks or even months either living apart while your husband looks for accommodation or living in hotels while you search for a house.

And when you do eventually reach moving day you can bet your life the husband isn't there. He's either out training or playing somewhere and you are left to organise the lot.

We have now moved house seven times since we've been married and Alan has never been present once. The worst experience I had was when Alan moved from Everton to Arsenal.

I was in the maternity hospital at the time having our second daughter Keeley. She was four days old on the day he signed and the hospital agreed to let me home early.

Normally when a mother comes home with a new baby the husband is there to greet her with a bunch of flowers and all the housework has been done. Not in my case.

Alan was off to London and the first thing I found as I walked through the front door of the home I loved were three cards from estate agencies saying: "We understand your property will be coming up for sale soon and we would be delighted to handle it for you."

I just burst into tears and that moment in my life was one of the few when I really cursed football.

It was not the only time I was to regret Alan's move to Arsenal. Although I later settled down to life in the South and now feel I do not want to move back North again, the first few months were sheer hell.

Apart from leaving my lovely home near Manchester, the biggest heartache was leaving my grandmother, who was eighty-six and had always been very close to me. The rest of my family understood why we had to move, but she couldn't grasp it all and for a time I was like a long-distance lorry driver, travelling up and down the motorway almost every week to see her.

Five months after we moved to London she died and I am convinced it was because she missed us so much.

There is an even nastier side to life for the families of football stars. It is when vindictive supporters start to take their dislike of a player out on his family.

The children get a mild form of this as soon as they start

school. The other kids soon discover who their dad is and quickly divide into two groups – those who want to become friends so they can go home with them and those who want to take the micky out of them and keep telling them what a useless player their father is.

For me the worst part comes when somehow our telephone number gets into the wrong hands. Then there's a series of abusive calls at all hours of the night and we have to change our number yet again.

And there is the odd occasion that really gives us the jitters.

Such an occasion happened during Alan's early days with Arsenal. We went on a summer holiday, taking the opportunity to have one of the few breaks we've had on our own by leaving the children and our golden retriever dog with friends who had kindly offered to look after them and the house we were renting in Palmers Green.

While we were away we received a message from them to say that the dog had died – but they gave us no specific details and we were upset but consoled ourselves that it was through natural causes. But when we arrived home we found police everywhere. They were guarding the house to protect the children because of what had happened to the dog.

It hadn't just died, it had been callously killed by someone and the police feared it was because of Alan's fame and that the attacker might not stop there.

I'm glad to say incidents like that have been very rare, but it is a constant fear and something footballers' wives have to learn to live with.

Another question I am often asked is: How do you get on with the wives of other footballers, particularly those in the same team as your husband?

I have always assumed that behind that particular question lurks the feeling that we footballing wives are always at each other's throats and that the rivalry that goes on inside the club is transferred to the wives.

But I can honestly say that in my experience this has never been the case. I've always got on well with the other

157

wives and have always assumed that we are no different to any group of wives with husbands in the same business.

Perhaps, on reflection, however, Alan is slightly different to the average player. Our closest friends have never been other players and their families, particularly not from the same club.

Alan mixes mainly with people from outside the game. I suppose in London our closest relationship inside football was with Bobby Moore and his wife.

I can only assume that Alan sees enough of his team-mates during training, playing matches and going on tours that he's looking for different company at a social level.

But that doesn't mean I am totally unaware of what is going on in his career at any given time. After all, I am usually the one who has to answer the telephone when the newspaper reporters ring with queries for or about Alan.

I think I've got to know most of the sports-writers over the years from our telephone conversations. Either Alan is out or doesn't feel like talking and I'm left to provide the explanations.

And the one call I'll never forget was the one that informed me Alan had been axed from the England team. It was very early in the morning and came from a London evening newspaper reporter. I was still half asleep but quickly came to my senses when he told me the news.

It was too much for me to take in and it was one of the occasions when I felt Alan had to take the call and hear the news for himself. I will never forget the shattering effect that news had on him.

I was so angry that Don Revie should have treated him that way. I had become as used as Alan had over the years to accepting disappointments, but this was one neither of us could take.

I was as proud as he was about his appointment as England's captain. I knew how much effort and worry and sweat he had put into that job.

I knew immediately that to lose it was the biggest setback he had received in his whole life and I felt helpless at not being able to comfort him when he needed it most.

All I could do was display my anger as vigorously as he

158

did to anyone who cared to listen. And I think that eventually my hatred of the England set-up went even deeper than Alan's.

Whenever an England match appeared on the television after that I was almost fanatical in my support for the other team. Alan knew the England players involved and instinctively wanted them to do well for their own sakes. But I positively wanted them to lose.

When I recall the shy lad I met on that bus as a schoolgirl so many years ago I am amazed that Alan has managed to be so controversial throughout his football career.

I always find it difficult to fit his face and character to the person I read about in the newspapers. Someone who seems to be in constant trouble with the establishment for saying or doing the wrong things.

I think that most of the time people just don't understand his complete honesty. He does annoy people, but only because he can't stop himself from saying exactly how he feels. I suppose you could say that diplomacy is not his biggest asset.

I often ask him why he has said or done something and he answers simply: "Because that's how I felt." He has complete confidence in his own ability and has little time for those who do a lot of shouting but have no talent to back it up.

But I must be equally honest and admit that he has a very stubborn streak in him. At times he can be absolutely pig-headed and if he's got an idea in his head nothing or nobody on earth can talk him out of it.

We never argue about material things, I don't think we've ever had a row about money, but we seem to have the same arguments all the time about our views on life.

We have the same likes and dislikes concerning most things, but there are just certain subjects that we never agree about. I keep putting forward the same argument and so does Alan. It gets to the stage when I say: "We might as well tape-record this and play it back now and again, it'll save us going through it all again."

Another thing that I find most annoying is that every so

159

often he picks up a phrase and continues to use it all the time. I think that is something peculiar to football. Someone starts saying something and it spreads like wild-fire right through the game.

Being alone so often should give a footballer's wife plenty of time for hobbies and other activities. But I'm afraid I don't take advantage of that.

I have no hobbies as such and just can't imagine myself getting involved with the Women's Institute or that sort of thing.

I was a hair-dresser before I was married and have often thought I would like to return to work in that field, but while the children are still young there's no chance of that.

Mind you, I don't get very bored at home. There's always something to be done because when it comes to the handyman stakes Alan is absolutely useless. He likes the garden, but only if all the hard work has already been done and all he has to do is keep it looking tidy.

As for jobs inside the house he's a complete disaster. One incident that comes immediately to mind should prove that.

It involved the house we owned in Manchester that I loved so much. It really was beautiful with old-fashioned beams painted in black and white. And there were a few other old-fashioned aspects, including a toilet which had one of those ancient cisterns on the wall.

I remember one particular party we threw, during which someone tugged the chain a bit too hard and it became detached from the ball-cock. I asked Alan to repair it and soon afterwards he assured me he had done so.

But as the night went on I noticed more and more people coming out of the toilet with a smile on their face. Finally I went in to inspect things.

Instead of just hooking the chain to the ball-cock arm, which seemed so simple to do in my opinion, Alan had decided the only way to solve the problem was to take a mop he'd found in the bathroom and tie it to the arm. So anyone flushing the toilet had to pull the mop handle.

I was furious at the time but finally saw the funny side of it myself. I decided to leave it there as a symbol of

160

Alan's do-it-yourself ability. We sold the house with the mop still hanging there and as far as I know it still is.

But what he lacks as a handyman Alan more than makes up for as a father. He is really super with the children. I honestly don't think they could have a better father in the world.

Maybe they don't see him as often as other children see their dads, but when he is at home he more than makes up for it. I think the greatest thing about their relationship is that they trust him completely.

He has never made a promise to them that he hasn't kept and they know that he will never let them down or allow them to get hurt.

I think the best example of this is that by the age of three both Mandy and Keeley were swimming because he told them they could and they believed him. And I'll never forget him telling Mandy as a three-year-old, to jump into the pool off the diving board. She was obviously frightened but he promised her that he would catch her in the water and that she would be safe.

She jumped into ten feet of water and Alan caught her hand and went right to the bottom with her and brought her up again. She's been jumping into swimming pools ever since.

That's the effect he has on them – they'd follow him anywhere. Really, he's just a great guy and I don't care who hates him. We all love you, Alan, and that's all that matters – whether you are a famous footballer or not.'

What Dad thinks of me

My father was born in Farnworth in 1925. He was the son of a Welsh father and a Scots mother and, like his father, he was christened James Alan Ball.

When I came along they called me Alan James Ball and now I have reverted back to the original by naming my boy James Alan.

It was my grandfather who started the football tradition in our family. He was a well-known amateur in the Lancashire area playing for most of the top teams and also for the county.

When my father left school the war had just started and there was no full-time football in this country so he became an apprentice carpenter, but football was always his first love and it didn't take him long to show his paces. There was a war-time League being run and, at the age of sixteen he played for Southport against Bolton.

He arrived for the match with his boots slung around his neck and the gatekeeper wouldn't let him in without paying. 'But I'm one of the players,' he told him. 'And I'm Shirley Temple,' came the reply.

Finally, the Southport manager was called to confirm that the sixteen-year-old red-head was indeed one of the performers that afternoon.

I'll now let him tell his story from there, as it concerns my life as well as his ...

162

Alan Ball senior writes:

'I was perhaps unlucky to have arrived at an age when I was ready to play professional football at the only time in my life when there wasn't any professional football.

But I was also lucky because during those war-time games at Southport and in the army I played with some of the great players that, under normal circumstances, I would never have been good enough to play on the same pitch with. Players like Stanley Matthews, whom I had a lot more respect for than young Alan did when he played with him.

Once the war was over I signed full-time for Southport and was then transferred for £7,500 to Birmingham. But I never really settled there. The wife was unhappy, and I went back to Southport on loan, or as they called it in those days, a "gentleman's agreement".

My next move was to Oldham and it was while playing for them in a match at Accrington that I saw young Alan score his first 'goal' on a League pitch.

He was only a little 'un but he had come with me to the match and had sat on the sidelines. I scored a goal and, suddenly, there he was racing on to the pitch and before anyone else could get to the ball he had reached it and proceeded to kick it into the net himself.

I suppose these days he would have been branded a hooligan and hauled off by the police. But things were quieter and more peaceful then. All that happened to Alan was that the referee lifted him up, gave him a penny and carried him back to the touchline. He was so full of himself, even at that age.

From Oldham I moved to Rochdale, a move which always sticks in my mind because out of the small share of the transfer money I was able to buy a television set. Television was new then and not many people had one. The one I bought had a nine-inch screen and Alan and his sister suddenly had a whole new world opened up to them.

At Rochdale I suffered an Achilles' tendon injury which put an end to my league career and the next step was into the non-league. I went to Oswestry as a player and then became their manager.

163

It was at Oswestry that I started seriously thinking about Alan's future in football. He used to come and train with the team. He was only ten or eleven but I could see he was a born footballer. In five-a-side games you could hear his squeaky voice yelling at grown men 'Play it square' or 'Give an early ball.' He'd picked up the phrases and mannerisms already and was full of confidence.

After Oswestry I had a spell in a pub back at Farnworth before managing another non-league side, Ashton United. And it was there that I decided Alan, at the age of fourteen, was good enough for senior football. His first game was on a Christmas morning and the opposition had a good laugh when they saw this skinny little lad lining up against them. But they didn't laugh for long.

He was playing at outside-right and the chap who was marking him got the biggest run-around of his life. In the next game Alan played against Earlstown, who were managed at the time by the great Wilf Mannion. After the game Mannion said to me: "That lad of yours is going to be a star, I'll give you £1,000 right now if you let him sign for me."

It shows what a good judge Mannion was. In those days Alan used to take people on and beat them with ease. I think it was Alf Ramsey who changed him into the player he has since become, but that didn't do him any harm.

My next move was to Nantwich Town where I led the team to win every Cup they entered for, and I was at Nantwich when Alan made his League début for Blackpool against Liverpool. I would have loved to have been there, but I had a job to do with Nantwich so, instead of being at Anfield with a crowd of 40,000 cheering my son, I was watching a match that attracted about 400 people.

I sent him a telegram wishing him well, and continued to do that for all his important games until he had played at least a dozen times for England and I felt he no longer needed my reassurance. But although I was not at that first game to share in his glory I'd had my own moment of satisfaction the night before the match.

I went up to his room to say goodnight and try to help calm what I thought would be his pre-match nerves. It was

164

about nine-thirty p.m. but when I arrived Alan was already fast asleep. If he was nervous he wasn't showing it, he was out to the world.

As I looked at him lying there, I saw his red hair glistening and he had such a calm look about him that I knew in that instant that he'd be a success.

I also knew that he would reach the heights in football I was never good enough to reach. "Tomorrow," I thought, "that lad will be playing in First Division football, and he'll be a star." It all seemed so inevitable at that moment, and I knew that everything I had done had been worth it.

Friends had told me my attitude was all wrong. I was too hard on the boy, never buying him toys, always ramming football down his throat. But they had not known the feeling that had grown between us during those years. I knew he wanted to be a great footballer and he knew I wanted him to achieve that aim almost more than he did.

I had total belief in his ability, he had total belief in my coaching. It was a bond that could not be broken and although I didn't dare disturb him, I wanted right then to pick him up and hug him and tell him: "We've made it, son."

My feelings towards him have not always been as emotional, as he has no doubt told you. And there was even a time when far from hugging him I actually ordered another player to deliberately go out and kick him.

It happened after I'd left Nantwich and worked my way back into the Football League as chief coach with Stoke City. Of course, the inevitable clash arrived when Stoke met Everton, for whom Alan was then playing.

I had always wanted him to do well in every game he has played before or since, but on that day he was the opposition, he was the one player in the Everton side that I knew could give Stoke problems – and, like the professional I have always prided myself on being, I decided that if there was any way of stopping him I was going to use it.

I knew Alan had a bad ankle which needed strapping in order for him to play. I told him a few days before the match: "If you play with that ankle you'll be carried off before the game is half over. I'll make sure one of our lads never leaves you alone and kicks that ankle at every opportunity."

As cocky as ever he replied: "Tell your lads what you like, they'll have to catch me before they can kick me."

The man I nominated to do the hatchet job on Alan was a tough defender named Eric Skeels. "Go out and get him," I ordered. "But he's your son," said Eric.

"I don't care. If we don't stop him he'll murder us. He's got a dodgy ankle already, a few whacks and he'll be off."

And sure enough everything went exactly according to plan. Skeels kept kicking Alan and long before the end he was carried off with his ankle swollen to the size of a balloon. What was even more important Stoke won the match and, at the time, that was all that mattered to me.

But although Alan accepted my tactics as part of the game and never reproached me for it, I had a terrible time with his mother. She was furious with me for, as she called it, "stooping so low just to win a football match as to order your own son to be deliberately injured."

She was so furious in fact that she left home and went to stay with her mother. It was three days before I could persuade her to return, and I had to take a bunch of roses and make a lot of apologies to achieve that. I'm glad to say it's the only time I've been on the opposite side to Alan. After Stoke I went to Manchester City where my job was to assess the opposition for Malcolm Allison, who I have always thought was a terrific coach and great for the game, and Joe Mercer, who taught me a great deal about the art of handling players.

From there I went to Halifax as manager and won the team promotion and then moved to Preston and did the same with them, before being sacked over an internal dispute when we were eighth in the table. But despite that I still look back on Preston as my favourite club.

From there it was off to Sweden as a coach and then back to Southport in an advisory capacity – at one stage I was working for them and the Swedish club at the same time. It was all a bit crazy really. Whereas most people commute from Stockport to Manchester I was commuting from Southport to Stockholm.

I was with Southport on Saturday afternoons and then spent the night getting to Stockholm for their game on a Sunday. I managed to do that for ten weeks before realising that my life was too short to throw away on that sort of schedule.

So I returned to Halifax. In my first season we had to apply for re-election, finishing fourth from bottom in Division Four, my most unsuccessful season with any team I've ever handled. But it was a challenge and that's something I've always loved.

Unfortunately I was not given the chance to meet that challenge for much longer. Football directors are impatient people and with the 1977/78 season only half-way over I was sacked. But there will be other challenges for me in the future. You've got to keeping fighting, you've got to keep trying to win.

That's the main lesson I hammered home to Alan every day of his life when he was a child. Life is all about winning, being content with second best is not good enough.

And I'm happy to say Alan has always tried to live by that rule. Whatever sport he participated in, his attitude has always been the same. He can't enter the arena without being a fierce competitor, always aiming to be the best.

He became a champion school cross-country runner and would have been a champion boxer if his temper hadn't got the better of him. He reached the final but got upset by something his opponent did and butted him. He was disqualified.

But there was one final when things didn't go wrong for him, the World Cup final at Wembley – the greatest moment of his life. And it was the biggest disappointment of my life that I was unable to share the marvellous triumph with him. I didn't even see the wonderful climax to that match with West Germany.

I had just started working for Stoke City at the time. The Stoke team had a match in Dublin on the Sunday after the World Cup final but we had all gone to Wembley thinking we had time to see the game before catching our flight.

But we didn't reckon on the game going into extra-time. When West Germany scored that late equaliser the Stoke manager Tony Waddington said: "That's it, we are off."

"But it's extra time," I said. "We can't miss that. I want to see my lad get his medal."

My appeal made no difference. "If you are working for us you are coming with us," said Waddington. And that's what I had to do. Walk away from Wembley leaving Alan and the fate of the World Cup behind me.

We reached the centre of London before I discovered that it was a winner's medal Alan would be taking home with him and I didn't see the extra-time dramas of the match until the following day in Dublin on a television set with shocking reception.

But as I saw the flickering picture of Alan collecting that medal I knew once again all the hard work I'd put into him and all the sacrifices he had made were now worth it.

There have been times since when I think perhaps that I still wasn't tough enough on Alan in those younger days. He continues to do things that baffle me. I think he's made a lot of bad decisions in his time, and the one that really upset me was his choice of Southampton as his new club when he left Arsenal.

Now I've got nothing against Southampton as a club. It's well run with an excellent manager and it's a nice area in which to live and bring up children. But when he moved from Arsenal they were a Second Division side and at the time there were at least two First Division teams who wanted Alan. He should have gone to one of them.

All other considerations, including the money aspect, should have taken second place to the one thing I had always hammered home to Alan – "Be the best." And, in football, being the best means playing in the First Division and playing for England.

The fact that Alan had been rejected, for whatever reasons, by Don Revie who was then in charge of England,

168

should not have deterred him from continuing to fight to get his place back.

And, in order to do that, he had to stay in the First Division. I was very angry with Alan at the time and I think what has happened since has proved me right. When Revie left and Ron Greenwood took over the England squad he was looking for a new midfield general.

He turned to Ian Callaghan, who was thirty-six. Surely Alan Ball, at thirty-two, would have had chances – had he still been playing at the top level.

As I told Alan when he first broke into the football scene: "You've always got to be noticed, make everyone know you are about." He certainly tried hard enough to do that but it could have been so much better for him had he had the right manager.

And in saying that I am not criticising any of the men Alan has played under for their ability soccer-wise. But somehow he has always been managed by the quieter men of football.

If he'd come under Malcolm Allison, Brian Clough or Bill Shankly, who would constantly have told the world what a fantastic player Alan Ball was, I don't think anything could have stopped him joining the ranks of the truly great players of all time.

Instead he's had the quiet and charming Ron Suart, the even more reticent Bertie Mee and Harry Catterick, who was not exactly the most publicity-conscious man in the business. So Alan had to do most of the talking for himself.

I always told him: "Son, no matter what anyone else thinks about you or your ability, the most important thing in life is to have pride in yourself."

I think he's always remembered that and I know I am certainly proud of his achievements. He still has weaknesses on the field, mind you.

I have always maintained that his biggest fault as a player was that he failed to pick people up at the back. It's no good just being a great player when you've got the ball, there's also a job to be done when the other side has it.

I still have a go at him about it when I see him play but he just shrugs and says: "Dad, you've been telling me that for as long as I can remember, and if I'm still not doing it I don't think I ever will."

As for his strengths? Well, everyone goes on about his work-rate and his refusal to give in on the field. But, as far as I'm concerned, anyone can achieve that.

No, for me his greatest asset is his ability to give a perfect pass, long or short. It took years of constant practice to achieve the degree of accuracy Alan achieves.

The weight of the pass is the secret, and Alan can judge it to perfection. The ball can roll towards the touchline, but somehow it just refuses to go out of play until a colleague reaches it when he is in full stride and, therefore, at his most dangerous.

Alan destroys defences with his passing and I still get a thrill out of seeing him in action. Whatever effort I put into his career has been repaid a hundred-fold by the sheer joy I have had from watching him succeed.

Whenever I see him play I say to myself: "What a lucky fella I am to have a son like that." ' '

That's typical of my dad, still having a go at me. But I'm still having a go as well and I reckon there's a few more seasons left in these little legs of mine.

I don't suppose I've changed much since those early days at Blackpool. A wiser man, perhaps, but still willing to say my piece and to hell with the consequences.

There is, perhaps, one aspect of my life that has changed. When I first arrived at Everton I was so hounded by autograph hunters I used to hide from them if I could. And if that didn't work I eventually became downright rude and told them to get lost. Now I've grown out of that petulant stage and, when it is convenient, I'm only too happy to sign autographs.

And when I do I like to add three little letters after my name. Not OBE or MBE, as some footballers can, but WIN.

I notice Malcolm Macdonald has now adopted the same gimmick, but I can assure you it was copied from me.

I hope that my attitude about winning is the biggest single factor in my life that has been brought home to you in this book. But what of the future?

170

The future

As I said in the opening chapter to this book, I am only thirty-three but as far as football is concerned I have lived a lifetime.

But I'm still enjoying the game, perhaps in many respects more than ever. I wonder, however, how many more generations of British youngsters will be brought up with the same love of the game or the same driving ambition to reach the top in the sport?

If the game is to survive in this country as we know it there has to be some drastic rethinking done by the people at the top.

I feel at times that those responsible for leading this great game into the future in Britain are far too remote from reality. I do not doubt their sincerity or their motivations – only their ability to see what is going on around them.

I have played the game in South Africa and Australia during summer tours, countries which are still considered 'babies' in the football world.

But I have heard more sense spoken by the rulers of football in those countries than I have ever heard over here. And we consider ourselves the 'father' of football. They are soccer crazy in both countries. They want to learn everything they can about the game, they want to improve.

And it's the same in America. The game is growing so

171

rapidly in the States I can see no way in which they will fail to succeed.

The Americans hate failure, and once they set their mind on something they will see it through to only one conclusion – a successful one.

They are already showing us the way it should be done – and we had a hundred-year start on them.

They are now taking the best players in the world and paying them the sort of money we in England can only dream about.

There was a time, not very long ago, when English managers going to America were considered mad. It was the place where the failures went. Now it's they who are laughing all the way to the bank.

But the Americans will not be content with just importing stars for much longer. Having taken the best from other countries, they will then start to produce the best. I think they will be a major Soccer power before many more years have passed. And where will we be? It's a terrifying thought that we could slip further down the ladder and finish as one of the minnows in the football world.

It could happen unless we do something drastic about the situation right now.

The first thing wrong with football in this country is that everyone seems only to see the bad things that are going on in the game. The image of trouble and strife is constantly pushed forward, no-one takes the trouble to write about the good things that happen.

I am constantly playing in charity football matches, charity golf matches, charity cricket matches. I enjoy them and feel content after them. I don't seek reward or even thanks. But it would be nice, now and again, to discover that somebody recognised the fact that it was happening. I am not alone, hundreds of players give up their spare time to do this sort of thing.

Yet all we get is the aggravation side of the sport rammed down our throats. The public seldom hear about the rest of it.

The next thing that should happen is that players be treated like normal human beings and not like chess pieces

172

to be moved around at the whim of directors and managers.

Freedom of contract is not just a throwaway, irrelevant phrase. It is vital to the future of football and I hope that by the time this book is published some commonsense will have prevailed.

I know that clubs have to cover themselves, there has to be some sort of compensation clause. But the player must have the right to move when he wants to. Once he has fulfilled his contract no-one should be able to tell him that he must sign another. He should be told: 'If you want to go and someone wants to buy you, you can go.'

I don't understand why the clubs have been so scared of this for so long. It must be a good thing for the game. The more movement there is of players, the more interest for the supporters.

No-one would lose, everyone would gain. So why has it taken so long to be implemented? It is just another example of the hierarchy trying to cling to power, and killing the game in the process.

Their attitude to sponsorship is exactly the same. Outdated and completely short-sighted. Why shouldn't large companies be allowed to sponsor football?

The Football League and Football Association seem worried to death that if the big companies move in, they will lose their authority. It's nonsense.

Every other major sport allows it, but the controlling bodies still stay in control. They just have fewer headaches from wondering where the next penny is coming from.

How would the money be used? For a start, something could be done to provide decent stadiums and facilities for the fans. I think most of the League grounds are a disgrace. I am sure every major city and town could put land aside for a stadium which just didn't cater for football but all sorts of recreations. A sporting complex that would be in use by the whole community every day and night of the week.

The clubs could sell their present grounds and, together with sponsors, build the new ones. Instead they stick to the stadiums that have been rotting away for fifty years.

Why should fans put up with rotten facilties and pay ever-increasing admission prices? They wouldn't stand for it on the Continent or in South America.

Let's get businesslike, let's put the game first and the behind-the-scenes power game second. Let's think like the Americans, the Australians and South Africans and make a fresh start. It's the only way we will become great again. Also our attitude to young players is all wrong. Allow them to join a professional club at an earlier age, let them be with the top professionals, watch them train then go home and practise what they've seen. It must breed better players.

But we are so traditionalist in this country no-one wants anything to change. They even scream with rage because of the change in our football shirts.

To me a shirt is a shirt. The colour or design makes no difference to my ability and if it means extra cash coming into the club, so what? Why do we have to look backwards all the time?

The glories of the past are gone. No-one can live on memories. The future is important, and the future starts today. So for God's sake let's get off our backsides and do something about it.

Postscript

Well, we made it. Southampton's promotion to the First Division last April was a great occasion for everyone connected with the club and a credit to everyone in the club.

Particularly for manager Lawrie McMenemy who had to rebuild his team after they were relegated in the 1973–74 season.

While rebuilding his side he also managed to win the FA Cup, which is no mean achievement. An even greater achievement in my opinion was that he refused at any time to sacrifice his principles of putting an attractive side onto the field.

Many managers, hungry for quick success, would have succumbed to using a safety-first policy—promotion at any price.

But McMenemy always went for the class players like Peter Osgood, Ted MacDougall, Phil Boyer, Chris Nichol and, if you'll pardon the immodesty, myself.

When I moved to Southampton in December, 1976, I reckon Lawrie McMenemy and myself were the only two people convinced I'd done the right thing.

You will have read that my father was so upset that I had left the First Division that he wouldn't talk to me for

175

weeks. And there were plenty more who thought that it was the beginning of the end for me.

Well, I've proved them all wrong. I was out of the First Division for only 16 months—and I enjoyed every minute of it.

When McMenemy bought me, he was quoted as saying: 'I wanted Ball for his quality and consistency.' I don't think I've let him down and he certainly has not let me down. He promised that he would build a First Division team within two seasons.

The challenge of helping the Saints back to the top grade appealed to me and I can honestly say I put every ounce of effort into it.

Since I joined them for my first Second Division match at Plymouth on December 27, 1976, the Southampton side has played 65 League matches. And I've played in 64 of them, missing only one through injury at Bristol Rovers.

I think I've earned the right to tell my dad and all my other critics: 'Told you so.' And I've also earned the right to play at least another season in the First Division.

After the promotion celebrations I left immediately for a season in America with Philadelphia Fury—another great experience for me.

There is no doubt that the Game in America now has a marvellous future. But my immediate future is back where I started with Blackpool 565 League games ago—in the top rank of the best League in the world.

Southampton's record since Alan Ball joined them is:

P	W	D	L
65	34	17	14

When he arrived in December, 1976, they were fifteenth in the Second Division. By the end of that season they had moved to eighth place—only eight points short of promotion.

Last season they finished second, only one point behind the champions, Bolton.

Ball's complete League record of appearances and goals now reads:

	Played	Goals
Blackpool	116	41
Everton	208	66
Arsenal	177	45
Southampton	64	6